MODEL 1911

★ Automatic Pistol

Robert Campbell

Stoeger Publishing Company • Accokeek, Maryland

Stoeger Publishing
Great Outdoor Books & More Since 1924

STOEGER PUBLISHING COMPANY
is a division of Benelli USA

Benelli USA
Vice President and General Manager:
  Stephen Otway
Vice President of Marketing and Communications:
  Stephen McKelvain

Stoeger Publishing Company
President: Jeffrey Reh
Publisher: Jay Langston
Managing Editor: Harris J. Andrews
Design & Production Director:
  Cynthia T. Richardson
Photography Director: Alex Bowers
Imaging Specialist: William Graves
National Sales Manager: Jennifer Thomas
Special Accounts Manager: Julie Brownlee
Publishing Assistant: Tina Talmadge
Administrative Assistant: Shannon McWilliams
Proofreader: EEI Communications

Published by Stoeger Publishing Company
17603 Indian Head Highway, Suite 200
Accokeek, Maryland 20607

BK0506
ISBN: 0-88317-295-X
Library of Congress Control Number: 2004104795

Manufactured in the United States of America.

Distributed to the book trade and
to the sporting goods trade by:
Stoeger Industries
17603 Indian Head Highway, Suite 200
Accokeek, Maryland 20607
301-283-6300   Fax: 301-283-6986
www.stoegerpublishing.com

OTHER PUBLICATIONS:
Shooter's Bible
  The World's Standard Firearms
    Reference Book
Gun Trader's Guide
  Complete Fully Illustrated
    Guide to Modern Firearms with
    Current Market Values

HUNTING & SHOOTING:
Advanced Black Powder Hunting
Archer's Bible
Complete Book of Whitetail Hunting
Cowboy Action Shooting
Elk Hunter's Bible
Great Shooters of the World
High Performance Muzzleloading
  Big Game Rifles
Hounds of the World
Hunt Club Management Guide
Hunting America's Wild Turkey
Hunting and Shooting
  with the Modern Bow
Hunting Whitetails East & West
Hunting the Whitetail Rut
Labrador Retrievers
The Pocket Survival Guide
Shotgunning for Deer
Taxidermy Guide
Tennessee Whitetails
Trailing the Hunter's Moon
The Turkey Hunter's Tool Kit:
  Shooting Savvy
The Ultimate in Rifle Accuracy
Whitetail Strategies

COLLECTING BOOKS:
The Lore of Spices
Sporting Collectibles
The Working Folding Knife

FIREARMS:
Antique Guns
Complete Guide to Modern Rifles
Complete Guide to Service Handguns
Firearms Disassembly
  with Exploded Views
FN Browning Armorer to the World
Gunsmithing at Home
Heckler & Koch:
  Armorers of the Free World
How to Buy & Sell Used Guns
Modern Beretta Firearms
Spanish Handguns
The Ultimate in Rifle Accuracy
The Walther Handgun Story

RELOADING:
Complete Reloading Guide
The Handloader's Manual of
  Cartridge Conversions 3rd Ed.
Modern Sporting Rifle Cartridges

FISHING:
Bassing Bible
Catfishing: Beyond the Basics
The Complete Book of Flyfishing
Deceiving Trout
Fishing Made Easy
Fishing Online: 1,000 Best Web Sites
The Fly Fisherman's Entomological
  Pattern Book
Flyfishing for Trout A-Z
The Flytier's Companion
The Flytier's Manual
Handbook of Fly Tying
Ultimate Bass Boats

COOKING GAME:
The Complete Book of
  Dutch Oven Cooking
Dress 'Em Out
Fish & Shellfish Care & Cookery
Game Cookbook
Wild About Freshwater Fish
Wild About Game Birds
Wild About Seafood
Wild About Venison
Wild About Waterfowl
World's Best Catfish Cookbook

WILDLIFE PHOTOGRAPHY:
Conserving Wild America
Freedom Matters
Wild About Babies

FICTION:
Wounded Moon

NON-FICTION:
Escape In Iraq:
  The Thomas Hamill Story

CONTENTS

3

MODEL
1911
MODEL
1911
MODEL
1911
MODEL
1911
MODEL
1911
MODEL
1911
MODEL
1911
MODEL
1911
MODEL
1911
MODEL
1911
MODEL
1911
MODEL
1911
MODEL
1911
MODEL
1911
MODEL
1911
MODEL
1911
MODEL
1911
MODEL
1911
MODEL
1911
MODEL
1911
MODEL
1911
MODEL
1911
MODEL
1911
MODEL
1911
MODEL
1911
MODEL
1911
MODEL
1911
MODEL
1911
MODEL
1911
MODEL
1911
MODEL
1911
MODEL
1911
MODEL
1911

4

MODEL
1911
MODEL
1911
MODEL
1911
MODEL
1911
MODEL
1911
MODEL
1911
MODEL
1911
MODEL
1911
MODEL
1911
MODEL
1911
MODEL
1911
MODEL
1911
MODEL
1911
MODEL
1911
MODEL
1911
MODEL
1911
MODEL
1911
MODEL
1911
MODEL
1911
MODEL
1911
MODEL
1911

INTRODUCTION

Since its introduction in the early 20th century the Colt 1911 has set the standard for high power military and police side arms.

The 1911 pistol is something of an enigma. A contemporary of the Ford Model T and Edison phonograph, the 1911 has outlived its competition, if indeed it had any. To this day the 1911 automatic remains a paradigm of engineering expertise, offering an excellent balance between controllability and power. At its best the pistol is as accurate as any other, depending on the ability of the shooter to manage the potent weapon. The fact remains that powerful handguns are difficult to control properly, while less powerful handguns are far less effective. The 1911's geometry seems inspired. The gun fits most hands equally well and has a feel of natural point not present in most auto-loading pistols.

The 1911 saw combat in Mexico during the punitive expedition of 1916. The pistol had been blooded in the Philippines, in operations against the Muslim Moro tribesmen, on the island of Mindanao, but in Mexico the 1911 was teamed up for the first time with elements of modern warfare such as radio communication, aircraft, automobiles and machine guns. In the near future the use of communications, automatic weapons and aircraft would change, but the Colt 1911 would remain a constant.

From a young age, I was in awe of the Army gun. My first exposure to the 1911 came from books in my middle school library by C. B. Colby. I don't remember them very well but they were gun books written for youngsters and they were good. I knew I had to have a 1911. I finally got my first 1911, a satin nickel finish Combat Commander, at the age of 13. It was among the first of the Series 70 guns. The first night I went on patrol as a police officer, I carried a Colt Commander in .45 ACP, loaded with Remington hardball ammunition. I would not be uncomfortable with the same gun today. Over the years, I developed a bond with the 1911. The gun is so good, with so many endearing qualities, that it builds that kind of loyalty. I have debriefed quite a few gunfight survivors. Those who used the .38, the 9mm, or the Magnum will say, "I did this" or "I did that," and in doing so, "I managed to survive." Those using the 1911 sing a different tune. They will look you in the eye and tell you, "The gun saved my life."

It is a different breed of weapon and I have little patience with detractors of the 1911. For the most part, they don't understand that this not a "he-man's" gun only or a weapon possessed of arcane properties. It is a gun that good men and women can use well. It evens the odds against our

The author often carried the 1911 during his time as a peace officer.

protein-fed ex-con criminal class or against murderous enemies of the republic. In untrained hands, it is a danger to all concerned, but no more than any other handgun and it is probably less likely to be involved in an accident due to its safety features. In trained hands it is a lifesaver without equal. The 1911 is used with excellent results in target shooting and pistol competition of all types and it is surprisingly effective as a hunting handgun. This is a book about a fighting handgun and how to use it.

Someone is bound to ask about my personal experience with the 1911. I have used the 1911 in competition and won quite a few trophies. I have taken game with the 1911. I have published articles on gunsmithing the 1911 in *American Gunsmith,* a reputable publication with immense technical interest. I have also covered the 1911 in *SWAT Magazine, Law and Order, Shotgun News, Gun Week, Gun Digest, Women and Guns, American Handgunner, The Journal: Voice of American Law Enforcement, Guns and Ammo, Handguns,* and other magazines. I have carried the 1911 for most of my time as a peace officer, and always preferred to carry it unless official edict stated otherwise. I know my way around the 1911.

I will share one incident from my career that speaks well of the 1911. This is from my personal notes. "…I could no longer move my left arm. I knew I was in trouble. I was muddy as a hog and with one assailant behind me, another possible adversary in the house, and an agitated felon in front of me, hoisting a blunt striking weapon. My Colt was in its thumb-break holster, immersed in soupy mud. The gun holster and even the grips and grip safety were caked with mud. The heavy leather of the holster was gouged from my fall off the porch, all four hundred pounds of men landing upon the point of my elbow. Despite the condition of the gun and holster, when the moment came the Colt came out quickly and sounded loud and clear. Had there been a need, it would have fired again."

The person behind the gun is most important but the 1911 is a good gun to stand behind. Read on and learn more.

This young shooter finds the 1911 good, fast-handling and accurate.

6

MODEL
1911
MODEL
1911
MODEL
1911
MODEL
1911
MODEL
1911
MODEL
1911
MODEL
1911
MODEL
1911
MODEL
1911
MODEL
1911
MODEL
1911
MODEL
1911
MODEL
1911
MODEL
1911
MODEL
1911
MODEL
1911
MODEL
1911
MODEL
1911
MODEL
1911
MODEL
1911
MODEL
1911
MODEL
1911
MODEL
1911

A BIT OF HISTORY

I am not a historian, although I have written on the subject in *Military Trader, Wilderness Way,* the *Gun Journal* and other publications. But it would be very difficult to support the arguments made on the 1911's superiority without a modicum of historical background.

When we look at the history of the handgun, we have to separate the shootings from the fights. When a mugger shoots an innocent victim or a helpless person is executed in a concentration camp, any gun will work. The mugger's junk grade .22 caliber revolver works well enough for him and so did the SS thug's 7.65 auto — neither are fighting pistols. Fighting pistols are used against other armed men. There is a difference understood by those who have the need for such a weapon. The first "handgonnes" were simple tubes loaded with shot or a round ball. Even after the first few hundred years of evolution, the handgun was only effective just past saber range. First issued as big-bore cavalry weapons, "horse pistols" were useful for drop-ping an enemy at close range in a cavalry

A young Matthew Campbell fires a heavy- loaded .45 Colt single-action. The 1873 Colt had quite a bit of power but was fairly easy for the shooter to control.

melee or for point-blank defense. Early handguns were feared but not highly developed. The first rifled-barrel flintlock pistols, accurate but slow to load, were far more useful for dueling. The earliest repeating handguns were double-barreled versions of the flintlock, or revolving-barreled "knuckle dusters," all heavy and ill balanced. Then came the revolver. Sam Colt's revolver was not the first but it was by far the best, and the world changed overnight. It is no mere boast to state than the Colt pistol made our advance into the American West possible. A good man with a sword could defeat a single adversary, perhaps two -- Cyrano's actions notwith-standing. But now a good man with skill and nerve became a threat to a squad of infantry. With a pair of Colt pistols, a man could wreak havoc and inspire fear in less well armed enemies. Later, when those enemies were better armed, the good man would still prevail.

The first Colt's were weak in power. On paper, the .36-caliber round fired by the early Colt Patterson revolvers looks about like the modern .380

ACP. In actual use, it fared much better. The soft lead round or conical bullets expanded when they struck flesh, producing wounds that were difficult to repair. In the days before antibiotics, such a wound was a death sentence. Many died under the surgeon's knife, while many more succumbed to infection. Many fighting men, including President Andrew Jackson, lived their lives with a lead ball in their bodies. The .36 Colt, however, was not as effective as a fighting handgun should be. While deadly, the effect on a determined enemy was not always immediate, leaving a wounded adversary with time to inflict considerable damage upon the object of his attack. The .44-caliber Colt Walker and its lighter descendants, the three Dragoon models, were developed in response to this problem. These guns were giants compared with the Navy Colt, firing .457-diameter lead balls at well over 1,000 fps. Large, heavy, and robust, these .44s were powerful, hard-hitting guns capable of greater accuracy than many muskets of the day.

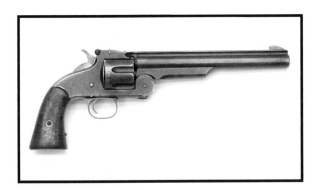

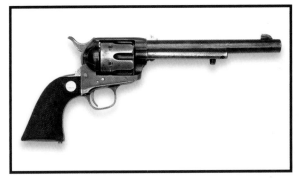

The Dragoon's chief drawback was its weight, a hefty 4.5 pounds, and Colt's lighter .36-caliber Navy Model revolver, introduced in 1851, quickly found a wide market. Colt offered a far better balance of weight and power in the Colt Army Model introduced in 1860. The Army was a lash-up in some ways — simply a Navy .36 with the frame slightly altered. The cylinder was rebated or enlarged only at the front. This permitted a .457-inch lead ball to be loaded over a moderate powder charge — the rear of the cylinder was the same diameter as that of the .36-caliber, to allow for the use of the Navy frame. Nevertheless, the Army model offered good power and acceptable accuracy and retained the Colt Navy's excellent handling qualities.

Colt's first powerful cartridge pistol, the Single-Action Army (SAA) breech-loading revolver was introduced in 1873 and saw extensive use in the Plains Wars and on the frontier by both outlaws and law officers. Some argue that the gun was already outdated when it was introduced since there were more advanced double-action revolvers and top-break models with simultaneous cartridge ejection available at the time. Few of the 1873 Army's competitors, however, were as robust as the Colt and none fired the powerful .45 Colt cartridge. The 255-grain, .454-inch conical ball, pro-

LEFT:
This top-break Smith & Wesson .44 was accurate but lacked the stopping power of the Colt .45.

ABOVE:
This 1873 Colt Single-Action Army revolver was the first Colt pistol to chamber the powerful .45 caliber metalic cartridge.

pelled at well over 900 fps, produced devastating effects when it met flesh and bone. The SAA handled quickly and the plow-shaped handle was very comfortable, even when firing heavy loads. A crisp trigger gave good hit potential. The SAA was simply a powerful, trouble-free handgun that could be relied upon. Anything larger would have been unwieldy in a handgun, while smaller calibers, although lighter in weight, were less effective. Double-action, big-bore revolvers are bulky and can be uncomfortable to fire due to the difference in frame design. No wonder so many western lawmen skipped the double-action revolver and kept their single-action revolvers until the 1911 became available. The history of the fighting handgun seems to follow a logical progression to the 1911, but there would be fits and starts along the way, as we shall see.

It is amazing that so many "firearms experts" question the historical record of the .45 Colt pistol. The Colt did perform as well as was claimed and the historical record speaks for itself. The evidence is there for anyone to see. Citations for valor, particularly those for the Medal of Honor are not given lightly. And many of those feature actions with the 1911. That the men who served our country would lie about their equipment is an assumption not well taken. The pundits who have cast doubt on Sgt. York's feat of arms would certainly never have brought the issue to his face when he was alive.

It is well known that soldiers tend to lose or destroy faulty equipment or even effective gear that they simply don't like. The Reising sub-machine guns that Marines found faulty in battle tended to get lost or dumped into pacific lagoons en masse. In England, British airmen equipped with the obsolescent American-made Brewster Buffalo fighter managed to wreck them all in training before taking them into combat! One of the reasons cited by able historians for the Allied victory during World War II is that after-action reports from American sources were accurate and contributed to the resilience of American tactics. Whatever the actions of the troops involved, and whether mistakes were made, they were reported accurately. This gave commanding officers good information to act upon. Yet many who claim the .45 Auto is overrated rely upon shadowy figures or "privileged" information. The case is clear. Good men used a good pistol, sometimes incredibly well.

JOHN MOSES BROWNING, FATHER OF THE 1911

John Moses Browning was one of America's most prolific firearms designers and there are few guns in use today that do not incorporate some elements of Browning's concepts. The son of an Ogden, Utah, gunsmith, young John was trained in his father's trade but soon became more interested in design, filing his first patent for a single-shot rifle in 1879. During his long career he designed military firearms such as the Browning Automatic Rifle, several .30-caliber machine guns, the first .50-caliber machine gun, and experimental multibarrel weapons that were precursors of the Vulcan Mini Gun. He also designed the popular Winchester 1894 lever-action rifle and the Browning A-5 automatic shotgun. Interested in self-loading rifles, Browning devised a means to harness the energy of the gas produced by discharged cartridges, allowing for the manufacture of semiautomatic sporting guns and fully automatic military firearms. His pistol designs used a short recoil system, harnessing the power of recoil to operate the mechanism. Ultimately, Browning's early designs defined the automatic pistol as we know it today. Prior to Browning's innovations, many of the working parts of most automatic pistols were exposed, as in the P-08 Luger and Mauser M-96 de-

This Browning High Power was a well-designed and reliable pistol with one main failing — the underpowered 9mm Paranellum (Luger) cartridge.

10

signs. Before 1900, Browning had devised a working automatic with a slide that enclosed the barrel and firing pin, and both Colt and Fabrique Nationale (FN) of Belgium produced his pistols.

Browning's Model 1900 Colt resembles the 1911 in some ways but is not as mature a design. The 1900 used barrel links both front and rear, allowing the barrel to tilt during recoil. The Browning recoil system works as follows. When the gun is fired, the slide and barrel recoil a certain distance together. They remain locked together to contain the pressure of the propellant. When the bullet leaves the barrel and the pressure reduces, the slide and barrel un-

Some years ago, when on special assignment, the author often carried these two examples of Browning's designs, the Browning High Power (top) and the Colt 1911 (bottom).

lock. The barrel is stopped by the rearward action of a pivoting link and the slide continues to the rear. An extractor mounted in the slide pulls the spent case from the chamber. A frame-mounted ejector thumps the case out of the slide window. A magazine spring then feeds the next round up, and the returning slide rams the cartridge into place. It works much quicker than the eye can follow and works reliably.

The first automatic pistols designed by Browning were chambered for the .38 ACP cartridge. The .38 Auto was a hot number for the time. Figures vary, but I have clocked original ammunition at as fast as 1,124 fps. This is with a 130-grain full-metal-jacketed bullet. As a comparison, the .38-caliber Colt military revolver cartridge threw a 152-grain bullet at just 752 fps. The .38 Special used a heavier 158-grain bullet but was only slightly more powerful. When the military began to shop for a self-loading pistol, Browning began work on a .45-caliber design. He steadily updated his design, eliminating the second link and increasing the caliber to .45, while maintaining a .900-inch-long cartridge case. A slide lock safety and the grip safety were added. The cavalry was a tremendously influential branch of the Army at the time, and cavalry planners

The grip safety and slide lock safety of the 1911 are just as important today as they were nearly one hundred years ago.

wanted the option of carrying the gun cocked and unlocked if need be. The grip safety was to be their fail-safe. The horse soldiers also insisted on a pistol that could be manipulated with one hand, allowing the trooper to keep control of the horse with the other. Much of the subsequent success of the 1911 is owed to these forward thinking cavalrymen. Browning designed the grip safety in order to satisfy the safety requirements put forth by US Army. As it turns out, generations of professionals have come to appreciate and re-discover the qualities that made the 1911 such a capable pistol.

U.S. ARMY TESTING

11

MODEL 1911
MODEL 1911
MODEL 1911
MODEL 1911
MODEL 1911
MODEL 1911
MODEL 1911
MODEL 1911
MODEL 1911
MODEL 1911
MODEL 1911
MODEL 1911
MODEL 1911
MODEL 1911
MODEL 1911
MODEL 1911
MODEL 1911
MODEL 1911
MODEL 1911
MODEL 1911
MODEL 1911

The U.S. Army ordnance planners knew exactly what they wanted. They sought to move into the modern world, fielding a semiautomatic pistol. That pistol would fire a cartridge similar to the .45 Colt if not quite as powerful. It is interesting that Great Britain, a country with considerable combat experience with aboriginal tribes and irregular warfare, adopted and maintained big-bore revolvers until just before World War II. Although Britain's powerful automatic, the .455 Webley-Scott, issued to the Royal Navy and Royal Flying Corps, did not prosper for several reasons, its .455 Webley cartridge would be chambered in British-purchased Colts.

In 1904, Chief of Army Ordnance Brigadier General William Crozier assigned infantry Captain John T. Thompson and Major Louis A. LaGarde of the Medical Corps, to investigate and recommend a new caliber of ammunition to be used in a new service handgun. Several types of handguns and ammunition styles were tested at a stockyard in Chicago on both live cattle and medical cadavers. Thompson and LaGarde concluded that "a bullet, which will have the shock effect and stopping effect at short ranges necessary for a military pistol or revolver, should have a caliber not less than .45."

The Savage .45-caliber automatic pistol, offered for testing during the 1907 Army trials, was not successful.

In 1905, with military trials in the offing, Colt asked John Browning to make improvements to his 1902 Military pistol design. Browning first designed a .45-caliber cartridge firing a 200-grain bullet and, later that year, Colt unveiled the Model 1905.

The Army's trials began in 1907 and a list of requirements for the new handgun was issued. The new weapon was to have a caliber of not less than .45, a magazine that carried no fewer than six rounds, a bullet weight of not less than 230 grains, and a trigger pull of not less than six pounds. Colt, Savage, DWM/Luger, Knoble, Bergmann, White-Merril, and Webley all provided entries. Many patterns were quickly rejected leaving only Colt, DWM, and Savage, but with each firm's pistol still in need of modifications. The Army then planned a one-year field trial to begin late in 1908.

12

Colt and Savage provided modified designs to the Chief of Ordnance for inspection, and in the spring of 1909, the pistols were issued to cavalry units for field trials.

The final variants of the Colt and Savage automatics were tested in March 1911. According to the rules of the test each gun would have to fire 6,000 rounds, with cleaning after every 100 shots fired. The guns would then be allowed to cool for five minutes. The guns would also be cleaned and oiled every 1,000 rounds. The gun was immersed in sand and mud during various stages. During actual testing, the pistol was dunked in a water bucket when it became too hot to hold. The Colt 1911 passed the grueling test with flying colors. On March 28, 1911, the U.S. Army adopted the Browning-designed Colt pistol as the United States Pistol, Caliber .45, Model 1911.

The original gun is instantly recognizable as the 1911 we know today. It weighed 40 ounces, was 8¼ inches long and 5¼ inches tall. The magazine held seven rounds, and the sights were relatively small and of a military type. The grips were checkered walnut. The original Colt featured a flat mainspring housing and a longer trigger than the later 1911A1. These trails were quite impressive in their day. I doubt any revolver today would go that many rounds without problems, especially considering the quality of ammunition available. The Colt was off to an auspicious beginning.

TOP:
An original 7½ inch-barrel SAA Colt and a modern Springfield .45. The .45-caliber revolver is slightly more powerful than the auto, when fired with proper loads.

BOTTOM:
Argentina adopted the Modelo 1927, a licensed copy of the Colt 1911, largely on the strength of U.S. Army testing.

ORIGINS AND THE FIRST ACTIONS

We can only imagine the reaction of the first troops issued the Colt 1911. The 1911 differed radically from the .38- and .45-caliber service revolvers that the soldiers had carried in earlier campaigns. The new automatic was not only self-feeding, but it automatically ejected spent cases, which the revolver did not do. The 1911 chambered a new round and cocked itself with each shot, allowing the solider to concentrate on marksmanship and fighting. Soon the 1911 would see use in the theater that in many ways had given it birth.

The action in the Philippines was the fiercest guerilla conflict that American troops had faced since the Seminole campaigns of the mid-nineteenth century. During the Moro rebellions, fought on the heels of the desperate fighting of the Philippine Insurrection, Americans faced an Islamic Jihad for the first time. The Moros are a group of Muslim tribes inhabiting the islands of Mindanao, Basilan, and the Sulu Archipelago. When American troops moved into former Spanish military installations in December of 1902, the Moro sultans, who had fought a long war against the Spanish colonial authorities, turned almost immediately against the newcomers. Between 1902 and 1906, the Army launched several expeditions into the interior of Mindanao to destroy Moro strongholds. It was not until June 1913 that U.S. Regulars finally defeated the last Moro holdouts at Mount Bagsac on Jolo Island.

A Marine practices with his 1911 between the wars. As part of the Navy, the Marine Corps adopted the 1911 in common with the other armed services.

14

The Moros were known for their ferocity in battle. In 1904 an American official called them "the wildest and most savage people on the face of the globe today." Dedicated suicide warriors, called "amoks" or "juramentados" by the Filipinos, launched one-man attacks to kill Christian enemies or die in the attempt. A War Department report of 1907 reported that the "Moros, men and women, were all fanatics, sworn to die rather than to yield, and certain, as they believed, of a glorious reward in the world to come if they died killing Christians." Protected by horn or chain mail armor, a fanatic Moro warrior, equipped with a charm warranted to make him invulnerable to American bullets and wielding his double-edged kris or two-handed kampilan, was a hard man to stop.

Pistols saw considerable use in the Philippines due to the nature of the occupation. When engaged in back-area chores or administrative duties, all soldiers carried a pistol. It was simply inconvenient to carry a long arm at all times. Rear areas were often the place of ambush and Moro suicide fighters attempted to disrupt and terrify American troops in supposedly peaceful rear areas. In one incident reported by historian David S Woodman, "A juramentado at Zamboango, hit in seven different places by revolver shots, nevertheless reached an American officer and sliced off one of his legs." Unfortunately, however, the pistol provided by the government, had severe shortcomings.

The .38 caliber Colt Model 1892 Revolver was the standard service side arm for U.S. forces during the Spanish-American War and Philippine-Insurrection.

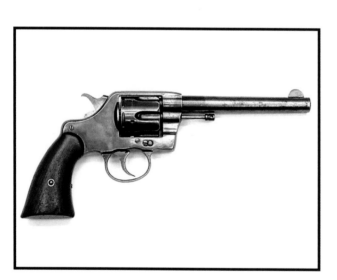

Just prior to the Spanish-American War, the Navy and then the Army had adopted the rather sorry .38-caliber Colt Model 1892 revolver. Not only was the caliber weak, the Model 1892 was not a robust design. Related in design to the Colt Lightning, a somewhat fragile double-action weapon with a poor reputation, the 1892 proved susceptible to going out of time and suffered from other malfunctions. Judging from period photos and reports, it seems that many soldiers chose to equip themselves with robust Colt SAAs in preference to the underpowered and fragile .38s. Private William Profitt, fighting earlier in Cuba, reported that he laid down his rifle and went to retrieve a nice-looking pearl-handled machete from the battleground when a Spaniard "jumped" him. Profitt drew and fired his .45 SAA and reported, "I was glad to have that old .45. Just a couple of shots and he went down for good."

Others, like Webb Hayes, the son of former President Rutherford B. Hayes, carried one of the double-action Colt .45s during their time in the Philippines. And the governor of the Moro Province, General Leonard Wood, is known to have carried a Smith & Wesson .44-caliber double-action revolver. At the time there were no modern double-action, swing-out-cylinder big-bore revolvers available, so men of action used the SAA or double-action revolvers of the same basic pattern. Hayes' .45 was a double-action or trigger-cocking revolver but the cartridges had to be loaded and ejected one round at a time. The top-break Smith & Wesson double-actions fired a much weaker .44-caliber cartridge, but offered simultaneous ejection of fired cartridges.

Sergeant Matt T McGhee of the Rough Riders argued that the Army .38 was worthless and had harsh words for the loading system of the Army's .30-caliber Krag rifle, another problematic weapon. The Army found that the Krag-Jorgensen rifle, with its relatively slow blunt bullet was a poor performer. Its side-loading magazine system was awkward. One soldier wryly remarked upon the cartridges spilled and dropped during attempted rapid loading as "sparkling in the sun."

While the influence of the Moro wars on the Army's decision to adopt the .45 has been questioned by some modern writers, the fact remains that the Army had adopted a cartridge that was too small to be effective and, as an expedient, brought back a fight-stopping cartridge, and ultimately produced a superior, more modern version of the same cartridge. The need to stop a determined adversary was very real, and the performance of the .38 was disappointing and occasionally fatal.

The 1911 .45 auto saw its first major action in the Philippines in June 1913 at Bud Bagsak. American forces assaulted the Moro fortress complex of Bagsak, a rugged mountain peak that had become the rendezvous for the outlaw element of all of the southern islands. Under the command of General John J. Pershing, men of the U.S. 8th Infantry and the 51st and 52nd Companies of Philippine Scouts supported by a company of mountain guns stormed and captured the ring of formidable cottas (forts) that guarded the massive stone fortress of Bagsak. About 500 Moros occupied the cottas at Bagsak and with few exceptions they fought to the death. After Bagsak, no complaints were registered about the 1911 — at least none by American soldiers.

MEXICO 1914-1917

Mexico was involved in a violent revolution prior to the First World War, with political and military turmoil spilling across the border into the United States. As early as 1913, U.S. Army forces stood ready at the border to intervene and assist American citizens in peril. In early 1914, following a dispute over the arrest of U.S. sailors by officials in Veracruz, troops occupied the city. The problem was quickly settled and the Navy withdrew. Civil war and anarchy continued in Mexico with four separate revolutionary governments claiming to represent the will of the people. Ultimately Venustiano Carranza emerged victorious and his government was soon

The grips on this 1911A1 feature the eagle and serpent of Mexico's national symbol.

recognized by the United States. Carranza's forces were supplied with munitions abandoned when U.S. forces left Veracruz.

One result of President Wilson's recognition of the Carranza government was to create an enemy in Carranza's opponent, Pancho Villa. The worst affront came in 1916 when Villa and his bandits, numbering perhaps 1,000 men, raided Columbus, New Mexico. The U.S. Army repelled the raiders but some 24 Americans were killed. General John "Blackjack" Pershing was sent to punish the bandits. For the first time, an American Aero Squadron was sent into action. For the most part, these aircraft were armed with .45 autos and nothing else!

Photographs of U.S. soldiers serving in Mexico clearly show the 1911 was in use by most of the troops. Among the actions that occurred during this time was a fight now known as the "last charge." Major Robert L. Howze commanded the 2nd Squadron (provisional) of the 11th U.S. Cavalry. While on patrol, the Cavalry was attacked at Ojo Azules by Villa's bandits. Howze's men made a valiant cavalry charge against the odds, and in the end 42 Villaistas were killed with no U.S. casualties. The battle raged for two hours, so there was certainly rifle work, but the 1911 was the weapon of choice during the engagement. The 1911 had been blooded, but the greatest challenge was yet to come.

THE GREAT WAR

When American troops arrived in Europe they carried beautifully crafted 1911s made at Colt and the Springfield Arsenal. Those 1911s played a role in the American combat experience in France and, by the armistice of November 11, 1918, the .45 had truly been through a trial by fire. Here are but a few stories of 1911 use during the Great War.

The last time anyone saw Marine Lieutenant Overton he was leading his troops into action with a cane in one hand, his .45 in the other. Private John Kelly, USMC, gave a whooping Indian war cry and threw a grenade into a German machine gun nest, shocking and killing some of the men inside. He then shot another German with his .45 Colt 1911 and the eight surviving machine-gunners surrendered. Kelly was awarded the Congressional Medal of Honor. Frank Luke of the Air Corps, the Arizona balloon buster, was shot down over German territory and fought to the last reportedly opening fire with his .45 automatic at 50 yards on the Germans who came to take him prisoner.

By far the best-known hero of World War One was Sergeant Alvin C. York. A corporal at the time of his exploits, York was a straightforward Christian soldier of unquestioned principles. York was engaged in an action in which he took out several enemy machine gun nests with rifle fire. He killed at least 25 of the enemy that day, and would capture 132. At one point, his rifle became too hot to fire and York turned his .45 against attacking German infantrymen. He fired seven rounds and stopped all seven men with one shot each.

Ultimately the 1911 would go on to set an equally impressive record in bush wars in Haiti and Nicaragua, during World War II in Europe and the islands of the Pacific, and in Korea and Vietnam.

This Model 1911 was manuafactured by the U.S. Armory in Springfield, Massachusetts. The government arsenal produced nearly 26,000 1911s between 1914 and 1917.

18

MODEL
1911
MODEL
1911
MODEL
1911
MODEL
1911
MODEL
1911
MODEL
1911
MODEL
1911
MODEL
1911
MODEL
1911
MODEL
1911
MODEL
1911
MODEL
1911
MODEL
1911
MODEL
1911
MODEL
1911
MODEL
1911
MODEL
1911
MODEL
1911
MODEL
1911

IMPROVEMENTS

After the Great War, ordnance planners determined that certain short-comings of the 1911 needed to be addressed. These related to how the Colt fit most people's hands — especially those with small hands. These changes were effective and gave us the Colt we all know and love today. The original trigger was shortened and two finger grooves were cut on

each side of the grip frame to make it easier for those with short fingers to reach the trigger. The mainspring housing was redesigned and contained in a housing that gave the rear of the grip a pronounced arch. This raised the bore axis of the 1911, reducing the tendency of the old 1911 Colt to shoot low.

The long hammer spur and the short-grip safety tang made cuts on some hands when the slide recoiled and, in response, the grip safety was changed. A longer hammer was also added, working in conjunction with the new grip safety to help eliminate hammer bite. The sights were changed slightly. These changes are reversible, except for the finger slashes in the frame. The 1911A1 format turned out to be the best for most shooters — once again Uncle Sam got it right.

Perhaps the greatest improvement in the 1911 line began during World War I. In order to speed delivery to the troops, several contractors undertook the manufacture of 1911 pistols. Contracts were signed with Remington, the National Cash Register Company, Savage, Burroughs Adding Machine, Winchester, the Lanston Monotype Company, North American Arms, and Caron Brothers of Canada. Only Remington, however, was able to produce any significant numbers of pistols before the war ended in 1918.

The 1911A1 included several design changes including finger cut-outs in the frame, an arched mainspring housing, and a shortened trigger.

Despite manufacturing shortfalls, the program set the stage for the first "clone" guns. Unlike many modern copies of the Colt, these were true clones, built from government-supplied drawings and specifications. At first Colt was to supply the drawings but could supply few accurate drawings. This was the beginning of 1911 manufacture to true military specification. Although some regard "mil spec" guns as somehow stripped down or less nicely finished 1911 pistols, the production values demanded by military contract were demanding. Complete interchangeability was required and government inspectors walked the various 1911 plants with tools and gauges to ensure that there was complete compliance with specifications.

In the years just before and after World War I several other nations

19

showed interest in America's formidable military sidearm. In 1915 Norway purchased 1911s for issue to its navy and, in 1917, obtained a license from Colt to manufacture the big pistol. I have examined several of the latter and they demonstrate high levels of fit and finish. The pistol differs slightly from the Colt in that the slide release is greatly extended in order to allow easy use with gloved hands. The Norwegian model was produced until World War II.

Another variation frequently encountered in this country is the Argentine 1911. Manufactured in great numbers, this pistol served the Argentine military until at least the 1980s and possibly longer, being produced until the mid-1960s by Fabrica Militar de Armas Portatiles

(FMAP). FMAP produced several variants. The first Argentine 1911 was the Model 1916, a Colt contract shipped between 1914 and 1919. The Model 1927, made in Argentina under license from Colt in 11.25mm (.45 caliber), is simply a variant of the 1911A1. I have owned several and they have given good service; they are good guns of quality comparable to the Colt. They were once good buys but are now seldom seen on the used gun market. I was able to test fire a Model 1927 for the field tests section.

GUNSMITHS AND THE 1911

National Match competition began at Caldwell, New Jersey, in 1919, and grew into the Camp Petty matches in Ohio. Since the armed services fired these matches with the service gun, the Colt 1911, there was considerable interest in building a gun that performed better than the standard issue military pistol. As early as 1920 Colt representatives did a thriving business "tuning" 1911s at Camp Perry. The first National Match guns were built by government armorers for the Army Marksmanship Unit.

Then Colt introduced a National Match pistol in 1932. It cost 40

LEFT:
These modern 1911s, shown with EK Commando knives, display features from both models of the .45 automatic. The Springfield model (top) features a 1911-style long trigger and flat mainspring housing, while the bottom pistol features an arched housing and a short trigger.

ABOVE:
Norway adopted the 1911 automatic in 1917 after purchasing a lot of Colt-made pistols for testing. The Norwegian 1911 was manufactured at the Koniggratz Arsenal until World War II.

dollars, about twice the price of a standard Colt 1911. The internal parts were specially fitted, particularly the trigger action, and the pistol featured better sights. Not all National Match guns featured adjustable sights, but some did. These pistols were the forerunners of the Gold Cup National Match, which was introduced in 1957. But the first National Match pistols, especially those with the optional Stevens sights, caused a sensation. Even with the availability of the National Match pistol, many gunsmiths, both in the Army and out, modified 1911s to gain new heights of performance. Some early Army-made National Match pistols had alterations such as rubber front strap covers and plastic triggers. Match triggers and barrels and adjustable sights, along with many of the modifications seen on modern custom .45s, were first used on guns intended for National Match shoots. High-visibility fixed sights were among the better things to come out of the National Match program. Aluminum triggers made their first appearance on some of these pistols.

The Gold Cup National Match Pistol, introduced by Colt in 1957, was a much different pistol, with standard adjustable sights and a special adjustable "match trigger." The slide was also about an ounce lighter than the standard 1911 in order to allow the pistol to function with wadcutter-type target loads. These pistols are really collector's items these days.

I have carried a Gold Cup with excellent service as a carry gun, but would make a different choice today. The adjustable sights are out of place on a combat gun. The roll pin that holds the sights in place sometimes shifts out of place and should be replaced with a solid pin. This is something that should be done by anyone whose Gold Cup still features a roll pin.

My Series 70 Gold Cup National Match featured the same weight slide as the 1911. Rumored to have a lighter recoil spring to accommodate wadcutter ammunition, I found the part number the same when planning to order a hardball spring for my Gold Cup. I often carried the pistol on duty as a patrol lieutenant but came to prefer a stock 1911A1.

In 1929, for many reasons, Colt introduced the first new caliber in the 1911 line. The .38 Super, which continues to rise and fall in popularity, but remains an interesting if misunderstood cartridge. The "Super," as it is affectionately called, is a faster round than any 9mm Parabellum (Luger). It is approximately equal to the .357 SIG. Like the .357 SIG, the Super mimics numerous .357 Magnum loadings but does not truly equal the Magnum. The reason for the Super's birth was the advent of modern mechanized thugs. During Prohibition gangsters and hoodlums had discovered

RESULTS FROM AUTHOR'S GOLD CUP .45, GENERAL ACCURACY

This is a good account of what was available in 1983, when these groups were logged in.

25 YARD BENCH-REST:

Handload 4.5 Bullseye 200-grain SWC	1.25"
Remington 230-grain ball	2.8"
Remington 185-grain JHP	3.25"
Winchester 1967 Match 230-grain	1.8"
Winchester 185-grain Silvertip	4.5"

the automobile. The various revolver cartridges then in use by police forces were pretty dismal against light cover, including sheet metal. All of these cartridges fired round-nose or conical-point bullets at subsonic velocities. The heavy-loaded .44 Special, recommended by Elmer Keith, would of been a good choice, but only a few experienced hand-gunners even knew of the existence of Keith loads at the time.

The .45 ACP, with its full-metal-jacketed bullet, was superior to most revolver ammunition but not by an impressive margin. Colt realized it could easily chamber the 1911 for the .38 ACP cartridge. Both shared the same .900-inch case length. The 1911 slide had to be redesigned to house a .38-caliber barrel, and the ejector was made taller to reliably eject the Super's tall, thin case. The 130-grain, full-metal-jacketed bullet used by the .38 ACP would predictably have better penetration than the .45 ACP "hardball" load. But that was not the entire story. The .38 ACP is sometimes rated as producing 1,050 fps. I have clocked the .38 ACP at somewhat higher velocities, but basically the .38 ACP falls in the 9mm Luger range.

Colt designers elected to jolt the .38 ACP's 130-grain bullet to a full 1,300 fps. The cartridge case was identical, but was now called the .38 Super. A Super cartridge fired in a .38 ACP will probably not wreck the gun but it will accelerate wear. The .38 ACP will probably malfunction due to increased slide velocity.

The Super offered tremendous advantages over any other American-made handgun in terms of penetration. However, in the first review of the pistol in the NRA's *American Rifleman,* two other advantages were pointed out. The Super shot very flat, allowing shots to connect at longer than normal pistol range. The Super also recoiled very little for a full-power cartridge. A combination of reciprocating pistol action and the relatively light charges of fast-burning powder resulted in a comfortable firearm to fire. In comparison, the .38–44 High Speed, a souped-up .38 Special, produced more recoil energy due to the heavier charge of the slower-burning powder used and the non-recoiling revolver action. Of course, the advantages of the semiautomatic action were apparent in terms of magazine capacity, rate of fire, and ease of reloading. The Super enjoyed some popularity with the FBI and was carried by famed lawman Frank Hamer, the man who took Bonnie and Clyde down.

A second, but not inconsiderable, reason for the .38 Super's creation was to attract foreign sales. Mexico and numerous other foreign nations limited civilian ownership of weapons by outlawing "military calibers." Rounds such as the 9mm Luger and the .45 ACP were banned. Although civilians could own handguns, potential revolutionaries would be unable

ABOVE:
The link and barrel lugs on this Storm Lake barrel are slightly oversize and must be hand-fitted for best results.

BELOW:
This modern Rock Island Armory Super shows good combat accuracy.

ABOVE:
One of the author's modified .45s (top) and a well-worn and much-used .38 Super. The Super is fitted with a Kart barrel, which greatly improved the weapon's performance.

BELOW:
The debate continues today—the .45 auto or the .357 Magnum revolver for police duty and defense?

to supply themselves with ammunition from seized government arsenals. Handguns could be sold in these nations in 9mm and smaller calibers. The .45 ACP problem was more complicated, but the .38 Super solved the problem of 1911 sales in prohibited regions. The Super became very popular in Mexico and was the trademark weapon of the Federales.

A few years after its introduction, the .38 Super was eclipsed by an even more powerful handgun. In 1935 the United States was a nation of revolver men. Smith & Wesson introduced its .357 Magnum revolver that year. The finely crafted revolver was arguably the high point of Smith & Wesson production, offering the lawman an all-purpose revolver. The Magnum, which could load sharp-shouldered semi-wad-cutters or Keith hollow-points, was a much more effective man stopper than the Super, with its full-metal-jacket bullet. As a result, the Super's star quickly fell.

Further modifications to the 1911A1 came in World War II, with the majority of military pistols produced with a Parkerized finish and plastic grips. In 1970, the Mark IV Series 70 pistol was introduced. These pistols were given a general tightening of fit and the finish was improved. A special collet bushing, which tightened the fit of the barrel to the bushing and slide, was incorporated into government-model pistols. The Colt Series 70 remains a masterpiece of good design, possessing excellent workmanship. In the Series 80 pistols, introduced in 1983, we saw the first positive firing pin blocks or drip safeties. This was an improvement in safety and an answer to market pressure from SIG and Smith & Wesson, which had introduced firing pin safeties, and Colt had to follow suit.

In 1985, the compact Officer's Model Colt was introduced. This is a truly lightweight, easily carried pistol with many good traits. In 1992, Colt introduced two opposing pistols that filled real needs. The Enhanced Model offered improvement usually found only on custom pistols. The slide rib, an indentation in front of the grip-strap that lowered the bore axis, and improved sights were among the additions. The 1991A1 was a pistol more similar to the issue 1911A1. This pistol uses a round-top slide and is usually supplied with an inexpensive blue finish. The 1991A1 provides a budget-grade 1911 with Colt quality. Modern Colts are offered with special beavertail safeties and forward-slide serrations.

THE COMMANDER

23

MODEL
1911
MODEL
1911
MODEL
1911
MODEL
1911
MODEL
1911
MODEL
1911
MODEL
1911
MODEL
1911
MODEL
1911
MODEL
1911
MODEL
1911
MODEL
1911
MODEL
1911
MODEL
1911
MODEL
1911
MODEL
1911
MODEL
1911
MODEL
1911
MODEL
1911
MODEL
1911

After the Second World War, the military took a hard look at its pistol. There was pressure, even at that time, to adopt a standard NATO cartridge. The United States was able to push the .308 on our allies fairly easily. Most of them were tooling up for rifles to replace their aging bolt-action models, and it was a simple matter to adopt a new cartridge. But the United States would never be able to convince them to adopt the .45 ACP. Our European allies adopted a spate of new designs in 9mm Parabellum (Luger) at nearly the same time. The British wisely purchased the proven Browning High Power and the French came up with the quirky but reliable model of 1950. The Italians produced the Beretta 1951, a good, solid pistol that offered fine performance. Some officers commanding armed services that included modern jet aircraft, guided missiles, and the M-14 rifle may have felt that they needed a more modern, sleek automatic pistol. The chosen pistol might have double action or not, but it would certainly be in 9mm.

This Commander-length Colt has been customized by Florida-based Accurate Plating and Weaponry.

Without delving deeply into the history of the trails, two new handguns were introduced. One was the Smith & Wesson Model 39, which went on to commercial success. This double-action 9mm pistol was the progenitor of a myriad of Smith & Wesson auto-pistol designs. Colt's offering, The Colt Commander, featured an aluminum frame that decreased the pistol's weight to 27 ounces. It was available in 9mm Luger or .45 ACP caliber. The slide and barrel of the 1911 were shortened ¾ of an inch. The Commander was quite a good pistol. After looking at the potential candidates, pistol selection was put on hold for about 30 years. The Army decided they had plenty of pistols and the 1911 went on to fight in Korea and Vietnam. Quite a few soldiers owe their lives to the Army's decision to keep the old warhorse in action.

The Commander is the lightest practical 1911, in my opinion, and its popularity is well deserved. While lighter than the Government Model, the Commander has the same full-length frame, allowing a good firing grip. While the aluminum frame may not be as long-lived as a steel frame, it is plenty tough. Well-known writer Skeeter Skelton once ran a 5,000-round test on the

This older model Commander features adjustable sights and functions well with Sierra 185-grain JHP bullets propelled by a stiff charge of Herco.

Commanders. The pistol passed the firing test with flying colors. Skelton himself often carried one or two Commanders during his career as a federal officer. On the durability issue, the case is settled. The Commander will take more firing than most of us are willing to give it. There are cautions, however, and they should be respected. The Commander was the first short-slide 1911, and pistols with short slides are more sensitive to ammunition that departs from hardball specifications. The balance of slide velocity and recoil energy is simply different. Commanders seem more likely to malfunction with 185- and 200-grain JHPs than the full size 1911s. Some Commanders, however, have proven completely reliable with all types of ammunition. I have fired several that were accurate and reliable with practically any load. But care must be taken to thoroughly test each individual weapon.

The barrel and slide of the Commander is this much shorter than those of the the Government Model.

The main issue with the Commander is recoil. The gun is much lighter than the Government Model and kicks accordingly. It does not hurt, but muzzle flip and recoil are there in spades. You will not shoot the Commander as well as you will a full size gun. The Commander is a fine defenseive weapon but its performance must be kept in perspective. It is a good choice for concealed carry but for open wear, as in police duty, the full- size pistol is a better choice. Just the same, the Commander remains a wonderful pistol for concealed carry, one of the great under-the-jacket guns of all time.

When the Series 70 pistols were introduced in 1970, a new type of Commander was produced. This is the Combat Commander, simply a Commander model with a steel frame. Pistol expert Colonel Jeff Cooper argued that losing ¾ inch of barrel and the collet bushing for a weight savings of only three ounces was pointless. I agree, but quite a few shooters preferred the Combat Commander. It is just a bit easier to carry, especially in appendix carry, and nearly as easy to control in rapid fire as the Government Model.

The author fires a seven-round string in good time with his modern Commander. With time and practice, the Commander is easily mastered.

The 1991A1 Compact is basically a stripped Combat Commander, with a good reputation. I had one of these pistols modified by Accurate Plating and Weaponry, and the pistol is among the most accurate 1911s I have ever owned. It is fitted with WC Wolff springs and a full-length guide rod and I find that it is reliable with any .45 ACP load. The Commander is a fine choice, the Combat Commander less appealing, but they are all good guns. If you don't care for the weight and length of a full size government model .45, the Commander is an excellent choice. Learn to use it well and it will be a friend that will never let you down.

COLONEL COOPER

25

MODEL
1911
MODEL
1911
MODEL
1911
MODEL
1911
MODEL
1911
MODEL
1911
MODEL
1911
MODEL
1911
MODEL
1911
MODEL
1911
MODEL
1911
MODEL
1911
MODEL
1911
MODEL
1911
MODEL
1911
MODEL
1911
MODEL
1911
MODEL
1911
MODEL
1911
MODEL
1911
MODEL
1911
MODEL
1911
MODEL
1911
MODEL
1911
MODEL
1911

Colonel Jeff Cooper served with the United States Marine Corps during World War II in the Pacific theater. Recognizing that while the pistol is probably the least important military tool in the overall scheme of things, it can nevertheless become an important one in certain circumstances. Cooper set out to find the best ways to employ the weapon. Like Generals Jonathan M. Wainwright and General George Patton, young Cooper went to war with a single action Army revolver. As he recalled later, trying to reload that relic in the dark was something he did not wish to repeat. Patton also ran short of bullets in Mexico as a young officer. Rather than going to a 1911, however, Patton chose to carry two revolvers! Jeff Cooper realized that ordnance types really knew what types of pistol troops should have to fight with. He determined that the best fighting handgun of all time was the Colt 1911 .45 auto.

Jeff Cooper is far from a one-idea person. He experimented with a super-hot .38 called the Super Cooper, long before the advent of the .357 SIG. This cartridge left the Super in the dirt and I suspect it would do the same to the SIG or the 9 x 23mm. He experimented with other cartridges, and was responsible for the idea of the 10mm auto. Today, various .40 pistols and full-size 10mms are based on many of Cooper's concepts.

Cooper's conclusions are unassailable, as they are grounded in experience, experimentation, and logic. Simply put, Colonel Cooper showed that the 1911 is faster into action than any other pistol, more controllable than any other big-bore pistol, fast in traversing from one target to the other, and easy to keep in action. Some commentators felt that Cooper's insistence on big-bore cartridges and subsequent penalties for small-bore cartridge use in competition were unfair. Small-bore calibers were deemed minor calibers. Well, small-bore pistol calibers in non-expanding bullet

The author strikes the Weaver Stance with his 1911, as advocated by firearms authority Colonel Jeff Cooper.

loads are about as half as effective as the big bore, so Cooper's validation of the big bore is not without grounds. Today there may be better ammunition available but the big bore is unquestionably the better cartridge.

Cooper explained the benefit of the Colt's low-bore axis, which limits muzzle flip, and the excellent overall human engineering of the 1911. Speed into action and speed of hits were proven in competition. Among Cooper's peers were the bright stars and top shooters of the century. These men came to a consensus on what was needed to make the 1911 a first-class fighting pistol. A good set of sights, a trigger job, and a speed safety were the consensus. The trigger need not be light but it had to be smooth. If exotic bullet styles were to be used, the feed ramp should be polished and widened.

Cooper's story is best told in his own words; his many books are available and well worth reading. I was fortunate to have grown up during his tenure at *Guns & Ammo,* and absorbed what Cooper wrote. This wisdom, delivered in monthly doses, was invaluable in forming my own ideas about handguns. I was able to recognize the preposterous in print quite easily after reading Cooper's work. His breadth of knowledge and quality of research is held in high esteem by anyone interested in the 1911 pistol. I feel that the Colonel's words are sometimes fascinating and always worthwhile. There are others who worked with the man and he gives them credit in his writings, but none have risen to the stature of Jeff Cooper. There is a good chance that some of my fights would have ended differently had I not absorbed this man's experience and taken it to heart. I am by no means alone in this situation.

This Wilson Combat pistol can trace its heritage to the concepts contained in the writings of Colonel Cooper.

27

MODEL
1911
MODEL
1911
MODEL
1911
MODEL
1911
MODEL
1911
MODEL
1911
MODEL
1911
MODEL
1911
MODEL
1911
MODEL
1911
MODEL
1911
MODEL
1911
MODEL
1911
MODEL
1911
MODEL
1911
MODEL
1911
MODEL
1911
MODEL
1911
MODEL
1911
MODEL
1911
MODEL
1911
MODEL
1911
MODEL
1911
MODEL
1911
MODEL
1911
MODEL
1911
MODEL
1911
MODEL
1911
MODEL
1911

THE 1911 IN POLICE WORK

Police work is thankless and stressful and there is no place for emotion. Admittedly, the 1911 is a pistol to which many of us assign deep emotional attachment. Faith and a sense of history go hand-in-hand with the Colt. If we choose survival gear based on logic, can we therefore logically choose the 1911 as a police pistol? It is difficult to remain objective when dealing with the 1911. I have to admit, the 1911 requires good training and a certain depth of understanding to be properly employed. This is not a criticism but a fact. In this chapter I have approached the 1911 as a fresh handgun and tested it as if it were a new design. After comparing the 1911 to the best of the modern crop, I am even more certain it is the better choice. I didn't start out to knock anyone's pistol, but there are numerous guns on the market that are not even roughly comparable to the 1911.

The modern police pistol is often a triumph of the technical over the tactical. The selection of the lowest common denominator is too often the training target in police agencies. Underachievers are seldom shown the door. Many cops are about as interested in learning pistol-craft as most students are in learning about high school fire drills. Administrators don't institute training until they are forced to, with training operating in a crisis mode. All too often it seems to be cheaper to bury cops than to train them. Regrettably, most modern double-action-only pistols exist to replace training. Let's look at the major criticisms leveled against the 1911 and compare them with the performance of the double-action-only models:

Compared with the SIG P220, the 1911 features a lower bore axis, a short trigger stroke, and a positive manual safety.

At close range, with the safety on, the 1911 is ready to fire in a heartbeat but safer than any pistol that does not incorporate a manual safety into the design.

• The 1911 trigger action is too light and the gun must be carried cocked and locked!

The double-action pistol requires that two trigger actions be learned: the double-action press and the single-action press. Most double-action-only pistols have no manual safety. The Colt is easier to shoot well than either type and has an excellent safety that positively protects against discharge. When changing positions, the Colt safety can be placed on instantly without de-cocking or any other movement. As for the light trigger, a hundred pounds of force can easily be exerted by two men struggling for a gun. The trigger action does not mean much in this type of action, light or heavy. My Chief and I never touched the trigger until we were ready to fire. A heavy trigger action is no sop to poor training.

• The 1911 demands more training

The 1911 requires no more training time than the double-action pistol. The time spent teaching rookies not to shoot themselves with the double-action-only pistol could be better spent teaching the finer points of the 1911.

• The 1911 is too large for most females

The 1911's grip is smaller in circumference than that of any double-column magazine pistol, such as the P 226 SIG or Model 17 Glock. The 1911 grip is slim enough to be used comfortably by practically anyone who can shoot a handgun.

• The 1911 (.45) kicks too much

This is more a training issue than a legitimate complaint. The 9mm +P is more snappy, and certain lightweight polymer-frame .40 caliber Glocks kick more than the .45. For the recoil energy, with the weight, the 1911 is more efficient than many less powerful sidearms. It is certainly not in the .357 Magnum recoil class.

• The 1911 is too heavy.

This is a hard question to answer — the pistol is big and heavy, but this helps it control recoil. The Commander is an option but the recoil goes up. You get used to the weight and many find it comforting rather than comfortable, a difference those going in harm's way know and appreciate.

• The 1911 has a low magazine capacity.

Only hits count. You can't miss fast enough to catch up. The more effective cartridge of the 1911 makes ending the fight with one shot much more likely.

• **The .45 is not needed, the 9mm (fill in the blank with newest wonder cartridge) is enough.**

When it comes to survival equipment, only the test of science is enough. Quite a few young cops take reports from the popular press to heart because these reports are more interesting to read than FBI reports. The .45 is proven both in war and in civil incidents. Big bullets do more damage and actual damage is the only mechanism we can rely upon. Big bullets do more work than little bullets.

In a Tacoma, Washington, pistol test program that included an ingenious test board that measured hand fit, trigger reach, and other important geometric concerns the 1911 was the "hands-down winner." I think that says it all.

Many of the new crop of service guns, such as the Heckler & Koch USP at top, base their appeal on certain 1911-like features, such as the cocked-and-locked action and low-bore axis.

This 1911 is carried in a Gould and Goodrich holster specially designed for police duty.

30

MODEL
1911
MODEL
1911
MODEL
1911
MODEL
1911
MODEL
1911
MODEL
1911
MODEL
1911
MODEL
1911
MODEL
1911
MODEL
1911
MODEL
1911
MODEL
1911
MODEL
1911
MODEL
1911
MODEL
1911
MODEL
1911
MODEL
1911
MODEL
1911
MODEL
1911
MODEL
1911
MODEL
1911
MODEL
1911

HANDGUN GEOMETRY

The design of the 1911 allows even shooters of slight frame and size to use it successfully.

In situations that call for a quick response, the controls of the 1911 fall readily under the hand.

I feel that the Tacoma program was certainly an important series of tests. Perhaps some of its conclusions could have been predicted. Any test program that examines full-sized fighting pistols is certain to give the 1911 high marks. After many years of exploring the steel/somatic relationship, I am still impressed with the 1911. Blocky slides and polymer do not suit my tastes, and the 1911 places fit to the hand before magazine capacity, and function over compactness. Four or five well-delivered hits are better than a fusillade of misses. The 1911 allows a firm grip and positive handling. It does not have swells in the grips. A flare at the base of the grip aids in control while the reverse degrades and twists the grip. The grip of the 1911 makes the gun a natural extension of the hand. When under stress, with wet, cold, or bloody hands, the 1911 grip fits most hands well. Relying upon the Great Spirit and Cor-Bon is fine, but I prefer a gun that is up to the task when needed.

Trigger leverage is not often clearly understood by beginning shooters. Sight alignment depends upon a proper grip, and the grip and alignment can be disturbed when the hand does not fit the grip and the trigger is recalcitrant. Double-action triggers require that the trigger finger be placed above the trigger so the finger can sweep down in an arc and press the trigger to the rear.

Because the 1911 is a single-action design, the trigger press is straight to the rear. Small and large hands can use the 1911 trigger equally well. The user's hand will seldom be off center. To test hand fit, simply take a triple-checked, unloaded weapon in hand. Press your hand tightly into the back strap. The grip should be relaxed but firm as you press the first joint of the finger into the trigger. The second digit may find its way onto the trigger if you have long fingers. The face of a double-action trigger may be beyond the reach of shooters with average to short fingers. Compare the trigger reach and effort in pulling even a heavy 1911 trigger straight to the rear with the effort needed to grasp and control a 10-pound double-action pistol trigger. There is little comparison.

The grip angle makes the handgun fit just right in the hand. Some angles are rugged or seem off balance. A pleasing grip angle is a joy to behold and to grasp. Another important consideration is bore axis. The height of the bore above the hand is measured as the bore axis, usually from the top of the hand where it grips the handle, to the middle of the bore. The higher the bore above the hand the more leverage for the gun to recoil. The Ruger P90 and the SIG P 220 have high bore axes for auto pistols, almost as high as some revolvers. This allows more recoil energy to rise and more muzzle flip to be exhibited. In the case of the Colt, there is little leverage for the muzzle to rise, resulting in low muzzle rise and excellent control. The lower the bore axis, the more recoil is directed straight back rather than in an arc. The low bore axis of the Colt is practically unique among handguns. The only non-1911 types that rival the Colt are the Glock designs.

TOP:
The 1911 (bottom) is far more comfortable in the hand than many modern double-action pistols. The double-action trigger system of pistols like the Beretta 92 demands a longer trigger reach.

BOTTOM:
Compared with the Golan (bottom), the 1911 has a slimmer grip, lower bore axis, and shorter trigger reach.

COMPARING HAND FIT

The best 1911 pistols are those that preserve the geometry of the original design while incorporating certain improvements into the template. As a comparison, I carefully measured several handguns and the results reflect hand fit. Do your own test with the wonder gun of the moment and see how it stacks up.

HANDGUN	GRIP CIRCUMFERENCE	GRIP WIDTH	TRIGGER REACH	BORE AXIS
Beretta 92	5 $\frac{7}{8}$	1 $\frac{5}{8}$	2 $\frac{5}{8}$	1 $\frac{11}{16}$
Colt 1911	5	1 $\frac{1}{8}$	2 $\frac{3}{4}$	1 $\frac{1}{2}$
Smith & Wesson Model 10 revolver	4 $\frac{7}{8}$	$\frac{7}{8}$	2 $\frac{1}{2}$	2 $\frac{1}{4}$

32

MODEL
1911
MODEL
1911
MODEL
1911
MODEL
1911
MODEL
1911
MODEL
1911
MODEL
1911
MODEL
1911
MODEL
1911
MODEL
1911
MODEL
1911
MODEL
1911
MODEL
1911
MODEL
1911
MODEL
1911
MODEL
1911
MODEL
1911
MODEL
1911
MODEL
1911
MODEL
1911
MODEL
1911
MODEL
1911
MODEL
1911
MODEL
1911
MODEL
1911
MODEL
1911
MODEL

SAFETY AND THE 1911

Safety is for the most part a human consideration. But the 1911 is a safer pistol than most handguns from a mechanical and practical standpoint. The ability to carry a handgun ready to fire simply by disengaging the safety and manipulating a trigger that features a short, crisp compression is a great advantage in accurate fire. The 1911 is primarily a fighting pistol, but it is also a good pistol on practical safety grounds. Some of the features of the 1911 that are found in many pistols today were quite novel and groundbreaking technology when they were originally introduced. They still give an advantage today.

Since 1911 pistols lack a positive firing-pin block, there is some discussion as to whether they should be carried hammer-down on a loaded chamber. I recommend cocked-and-locked carry, but sometimes carry my 1911s hammer-down in the waistband, Mexican style. I also leave the guns at ready in the home hammer-down on occasion. This is safe because the 1911 has an inertia firing pin. In other words, the spring-loaded firing pin is shorter than the firing pin channel. A blow on the hammer cannot cause the firing pin to strike the primer of a chambered cartridge. But when the gun is cocked and locked and the hammer falls at the press of the trigger, the hammer strikes with sufficient force to drive the firing pin forward against spring pressure, firing the weapon. The spring then uncoils to its original position. Modern Colt 1911s have a firing-pin block that holds the firing pin in place until the trigger is pressed completely to the rear. A spring-loaded plunger butts into a depression in the firing pin. This plunger falls away when the trigger reaches its rearward-most travel. Often termed a concession to liability concerns, the firing-pin block was also an answer to market pressure. Competing designs such as the SIG P 220 featured firing-pin blocks, and Colt answered in turn. The modern "drop safety" works. I have seen a 1911 fall across pavement so hard it emitted sparks, but did not fire.

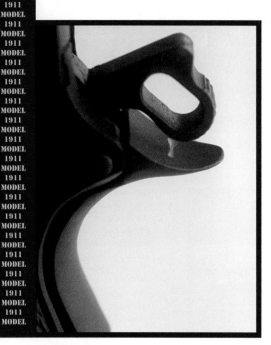

A unique and important safety feature of the Colt is the grip safety.

A feature that is much appreciated is the Colt grip safety. This safety is not intrusive upon handling, but blocks the trigger yoke until completely depressed. The grip safety moves in a shallow arc, balanced against the main spring housing, and it works efficiently. If the gun is dropped or the hand releases the grip safety, the grip safety springs to the rear, preventing trigger movement. Some 1911 variants such as the Star PD and the Star Super have eliminated the grip safety from their design. These are serviceable pistols but time has proven the value of the Colt-type grip safety.

The 1911 pistol (top) is ready for instant action, but retains a positive safety as well as a grip safety. The Glock double-action pistol below has only a lever inset in the trigger.

The slide lock safety locks the slide firmly in place when applied. This safety also blocks hammer fall. The slide lock safety blocks the hammer by blocking the sear and also locks the slide in place, doubling the safety features. In the 1911, the hammer is blocked by the manual safety and the trigger is blocked by the grip safety.

A hammer position missing from modern Colts is the half-cock notch. In numerous pistols, the half-cock notch is used as a safety notch. The purpose of the half-cock notch is to capture the hammer if the user slips while manually cocking the weapon. As late as the 1970s, I observed numerous gun carriers carrying a chamber-loaded Colt on the half-cock notch. This is not a wise thing to do. The half-cock notch of the 1911 has less meat in the steel than the full-cock notch. A condition known as false half cock can result from improper engagement, with the least amount of steel holding the hammer in place.

The Firestorm differs from most 1911s in form at but is faithful to the original idea.

The half-cock notch is simply an added measure of safety for those who carry the Colt hammer-down. It is fine as far as it goes, but should not be relied upon as a legitimate carry option. The half-cock notch is not a safety, but a safety feature. The 1911's combination of a manual safety, grip safety, and a firing pin block is unrivaled. The 1911 is a gun with design features appreciated by the seasoned handgunner.

This Wilson Combat grip safety has a bump on the end for sure engagement.

34

MODEL
1911
MODEL
1911
MODEL
1911
MODEL
1911
MODEL
1911
MODEL
1911
MODEL
1911
MODEL
1911
MODEL
1911
MODEL
1911
MODEL
1911
MODEL
1911
MODEL
1911
MODEL
1911
MODEL
1911
MODEL
1911
MODEL
1911
MODEL
1911
MODEL
1911
MODEL
1911
MODEL
1911
MODEL
1911
MODEL
1911
MODEL
1911
MODEL
1911
MODEL
1911
MODEL
1911
MODEL
1911
MODEL

CONDITIONS OF READINESS

The 1911 is by no means unique in having several levels of readiness: all auto pistols do. But few share the 1911's versatility in combat readiness. The first condition of carry is cocked and locked. This means that the hammer is fully to the rear and the slide lock safety is on. This is commonly referred to as "condition one." This is the proper carry when the 1911 is holstered. This carry allows for a rapid presentation and an accurate first-shot hit. Properly understood, in trained hands, cocked and locked is quite safe. However, there is a certain resistance to cocked-and-locked carry, particularly in police usage. The popularity of the LDA and SFS firing systems, covered elsewhere, is a direct result of the general fear or suspicion of cocked-and-locked carry. Cocked and locked is not recommended for carry in the belt with no holster, or for ready storage in home defense. But cocked-and-locked remains the way to go in a 1911 pistol. If you are not comfortable with cocked-and-locked carry, choose the LDA or an SFS-fitted pistol. With all due respect to workable designs, I prefer the standard single-action for my use. In some pistol designs the only safe carry option is hammer-down on an empty chamber. The 1911 gives us much better choices.

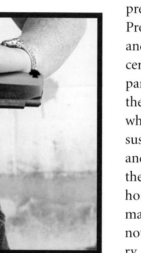

Some effort and practice is required to quickly chamber a round in an empty 1911.

The second condition of readiness is "condition two," or hammer-down on a chambered round. The gun is cocked on the draw prior to firing. This draw is fumble prone in my experience and less than ideal. With modern 1911s featuring the firing-pin block it is quite safe, but the gun should not be cocked until the pistol is well away from the body. Otherwise, a chance exists that the thumb will slip and let the hammer ride down to fire the gun. Hammer-down on a loaded chamber was often used by cops in my youth who wanted to carry the .45 but did not like cocked-

and-locked carry. I am completely comfortable with condition-one carry, which I regard as safer than hammer down on a live chamber. But hammer-down may prove the best choice for some users.

A third choice is "condition three," or empty chamber ready. This was the prescribed carry in many agencies that allowed the 1911, including the Chicago Police Department. It is quite safe, though slow into action. Surprisingly, I have found chamber-empty as quick into action as hammer-down on a loaded chamber, as long as both hands are free.

The major advantages of the 1911 are abrogated by hammer-down or chamber-empty carry. If you cannot live with cocked-and-locked carry or do not trust yourself, then perhaps another design would be best. The LDA certainly answers many problems. I have seen Federal agents, newly issued with Glock pistols, carry them with an empty chamber, simply stuck in their belts, without a holster. This carry is probably more popular than many of us believe. I suppose I would rather carry a 1911 in this manner than any other auto pistol in any condition of readiness, but then, do we wish to plow a field with a sick mule or a healthy horse? I'll take the healthy unfettered mule and carry my 1911 cocked and locked.

While both the 1911 (top) and the double-action pistol illustrated at left can be fired quickly, the 1911 features a short trigger press for great accuracy.

In some pistol designs, such as this Browning variant, the only safe carry option is hammer-down on an empty chamber.

MODEL
1911
MODEL
1911
MODEL
1911
MODEL
1911
MODEL
1911
MODEL
1911
MODEL
1911
MODEL
1911
MODEL
1911
MODEL
1911
MODEL
1911
MODEL
1911
MODEL
1911
MODEL
1911
MODEL
1911
MODEL
1911
MODEL
1911
MODEL
1911
MODEL
1911
MODEL
1911
MODEL
1911
MODEL
1911
MODEL
1911
MODEL
1911
MODEL
1911
MODEL
1911
MODEL
1911
MODEL
1911
MODEL
1911
MODEL

DISASSEMBLY AND MAINTENANCE

Anyone owning a handgun or a vehicle should be able to perform routine maintenance, otherwise considerable expense and danger can be involved. Routine maintenance and lubrication are vital. The analogy to a vehicle is an apt one. Vehicles need lubrication and spring replacement and wear is a constant with any machine that has moving parts. The 1911 is not as simple to field-strip as some pistols but poses no problems for the average person. Begin with a triple-checked unloaded 1911. It is important to keep your face out of the path of the recoil spring guide, a warning I publish first in any discussion of taking the 1911 down. For disassembly, I use a Wilson combat bushing wrench. A synthetic wrench is far less likely to mar the pistol's finish.

The sequence is as follows: Placing the bushing wrench over the barrel bushing, depress the spring guide

The 1911 is fairly simple to break into basic components — action, slide, and barrel.

and turn the barrel bushing carefully to the unlocked position. Carefully capture the recoil spring guide and place it aside. The recoil spring will now protrude from the slide. This is not a problem at this stage. Next, push the slide to the rear to the point where the crescent-shaped cutout in the slide meets the tip of the slide stop. The slide stop can now be pressed out of the frame. You may now run the slide forward and off the frame. Take care not to allow the recoil spring and spring guide rod to drop out of the slide. You can now turn the slide bottom side upward to remove the guide and spring. Next, turn the bushing until the retaining lug is free and pull the bushing forward. The barrel is gently rocked from its recesses in the slide and brought out the front of the slide. That is all that is needed to clean the gun. Reassembly is the reverse.

Some remove the recoil plug first and then remove the recoil spring from the bottom. Either method works. A number of 1911s, and almost all military specification guns, are loose enough so that the fingers are all that is needed to remove the recoil spring guide and barrel bushings. Tightly fitted guns, however, can require considerable effort. Some pistols, especially those with full-length guide rods, require tools to take down. Normally, the slide is locked to the rear, a wrench is inserted in the guide rod, and the rod is turned out — most are two-piece units. Many of the smaller weapons that use slides and barrels without bushings can be taken down by stripping the slide from the frame. This is all that is required for routine maintenance.

Be certain to carefully scrub the barrel with repeated brushing using a quality copper brush to remove powder and lead deposits. Use a good solvent—Hoppes' is well proven—and thoroughly remove any unburned powder and powder ash from the weapon. The 1911 is reliable, but a buildup of this grit can do you in. Lubricate the gun after the piece is clean and dry. There are some pretty good products for lubricating on the market but there are others that don't perform nearly so well. I think Rem Oil is among the best for all-around use, especially in very cold climates. It does not congeal in cold weather, as was shown by my test program. Birchwood Casey and the various other Gun Slick (Outers) products give excellent results.

I begin my maintenance procedure by dampening a cleaning patch with oil. I wipe the long bearing surfaces and barrel and slide with this patch. Be certain to put a dot of oil on the barrel where it bears against the slide bushing. The receiver rails should get a share of lubricant. The places where the long bearing surfaces rub together should always get attention. After lubrication, rack the slide repeatedly until the oil is evenly distributed. The pistol is fine lightly oiled for carry, but if extended-range sessions are indicated, a heavier coat of lubricant is needed. Depending upon the climate, it may be wise to check and lubricate the 1911 as often as once a week. It's your hide, but this type of treatment ensures reliability. When the pistol is disassembled, I also lube the bow of the trigger and the mainspring and grip safety engagement points, as well as the sear. I lightly clean and oil a 1911 that is on duty after every 500 rounds and thoroughly strip and clean it after every 1,000 rounds. Why do I do this when the gun will go 6,000 rounds without trouble? Long-term accumulation of debris is more hazardous than an intense-range trip. Again, it is your hide!

38

MODEL
1911
MODEL
1911
MODEL
1911
MODEL
1911
MODEL
1911
MODEL
1911
MODEL
1911
MODEL
1911
MODEL
1911
MODEL
1911
MODEL
1911
MODEL
1911
MODEL
1911
MODEL
1911
MODEL
1911
MODEL
1911
MODEL
1911
MODEL
1911
MODEL
1911
MODEL
1911
MODEL
1911
MODEL
1911
MODEL
1911
MODEL

MAGAZINES: THE HEART OF THE GUN

For most of the career of the 1911, the simple, sturdy, and rugged GI magazine was all that was available. I suppose some would expect me to put down these magazines and criticize them at this point, but the fact remains that they were fine performers. They worked well in hazardous situations, they fed thousands of rounds without failure, and were generally of high quality. They were not perfect, but were well suited to the intended mission. That mission was to properly feed hardball ammunition into the action and they did this very well. Many of the magazines available today are basic hardball-type magazines with various improvements. There are reasons that the original magazine needed to be modified, as we will see.

This early model magazine has given generally good service

One reason is that the pistols have changed. Today, my Colt Commander feeds practically any bullet style perfectly, but the magazine, and the Triple K spares I have for this gun, appear not very different from GI types. The feed ramp of the Commander has been modified and polished — a great improvement. This allows the use of hollow-point bullets with a wide-open cavity in the nose. However, there are many GI guns that will not feed hollow-points, at least not with the GI magazines. The problem first reared its head when target shooters attempted to use semi-wad-cutter bullets with blunt noses in the 1911. These rounds were loaded with lighter charges than hardball ammunition. The need, therefore, existed for a magazine that released the bullet earlier in the feed cycle. In other words, instead of bouncing the bullet off the feed ramp and into the chamber, the bullet needed to be fed directly into the chamber. This was necessary both to feed the flat-nose bullet and to allow feeding of a cartridge with less than hardball power.

Army gunsmiths simply bent and adjusted the feed lips of the GI magazine and they had a reliable magazine. They knew just how to do it and passed this skill on to others.

The Wilson Combat magazine is arguably the standard by which all others are measured and it is the ultimate development of this standard. The Wilson Combat magazine feeds the bullet earlier in the cycle and will often allow 1911 pistols to function with JHP bullets with no other modification to the gun. This magazine is an all-stainless unit, normally supplied with a rubber butt pad. I have had excellent service from these magazines.

Another brand of magazine that has given faultless service in long-term testing is the pattern made by Metalform. The spectrum of professional 1911 users seems to be divided between those who prefer the Metalform magazine and those who prefer the Wilson Combat. The Metalform magazine is a solid, rugged, and reliable unit that probably does not get the praise it deserves. I remember my first, and it solved a lot of problems in a grumpy Colt Commander that had been butchered. The Metalform magazine is available in a number of configurations, including an original 1911 style with lanyard ring. This is the only magazine I recommend with Officer's Model-type pistols. Buy the 6-round Metalform or be ready for malfunctions.

I have performed cursory tests on both Les Baer and McCormack magazines and each has given good service in my limited testing. There are other magazines that are known as "range magazines:" cheap versions for use on the target range. That is OK as far as it goes, but I don't mix them with service magazines. If you purchase a gun show magazine for five bucks and it has problems, this can lead to a lack of confidence in the gun itself. It is best to always use quality magazines but, that being said, there are several outlets offering good magazines at a bargain price. Pro Mag and Triple K are among them. I have used Triple K magazines with the Colt, Star, Llama, Beretta, Savage, Browning, and various other pistols. They are the only source for some of these types of pistol and have given acceptable service over time. The Pro Mag has given good performance in both the Colt and Beretta pistols. These magazines cost perhaps half what a Wilson Combat magazine costs. While they will not last as long and may not be as suitable for +P loads and heavy use, they have given acceptable results. Five or six range magazines for practice is a must and these magazines fulfill that need. I have three Triple K magazines that once were the only magazines I had for the Colt .38 Super, and they are perhaps 20 years old. They work fine, but

TOP:
The proper feed angle is essential when using hollowpoint ammunition.

BOTTOM:
These Triple K magazines, in .38 Super, have given excellent service.

This Metalform magazine proved reliable in feeding 300-grain JSP handloads.

The plastic component on the bottom of this Metal-form 10-round magazine prevents the oversize magazine from being inserted too far into the grip frame.

they certainly are well worn and common sense dictates that they should no longer be trusted for duty.

When it comes to the .38 Super, I have used McCormack magazines far more extensively than the originals made for this caliber. I had a balky Super that was off spec and causing problems. It was a prototype, one of the first production examples of this gun, and it actually arrived with a .45 caliber magazine in the frame! I was able to convince it to feed most Super ammunition after special-ordering two McCormack magazines. They cost twice as much as Triple K but they solved my problem.

New-style magazines in both .38 Super and .45-calibers use a rounded rather than a flat follower. This allows the cartridge to be held higher than usual, resulting in excellent feed reliability. This is coupled with a feed-lip redesign that opens the lip to encourage early feeding of the rounds. Coupled with newer-style feed ramps and barrel chambers, the feed reliability of 1911 pistols is much improved. It is also possible to improve GI-type magazines by adding a new style follower and premium magazine springs.

Magazines require maintenance as much as your pistol does. Magazines accumulate unburned powder and dirt from the range. Watch out for dents and any wear on the magazine catch hole. To clean the magazine, the base is pressed off and the spring removed. The follower will normally remain attached to the spring. The body of the magazine can then be brushed clean. The spring may have grit clinging to it and will need to be wiped down. The follower can also be quite dirty and should be cleaned. By taking these few steps, the 1911 will perform as expected.

The tests would not have been possible without a good number of magazines on hand. Function was flawless in the case of the new-model magazines and most GI types as well.

41

MODEL
1911
MODEL
1911
MODEL
1911
MODEL
1911
MODEL
1911
MODEL
1911
MODEL
1911
MODEL
1911
MODEL
1911
MODEL
1911
MODEL
1911
MODEL
1911
MODEL
1911
MODEL
1911
MODEL
1911
MODEL
1911
MODEL
1911
MODEL
1911
MODEL
1911
MODEL
1911
MODEL
1911

SIGHTS

It is an error to stay that the stock 1911 has fixed sights. The rear sight is adjustable for drift. The factory sights now found on most 1911 pistols are at least usable. The Colt Series 80 pistols feature high-visibility sights similar to King's Hardballer sights. These sights may seem simple today but are a big improvement over military-type sights. The Kimber standard model features McCormack sights, and numerous other 1911s feature Novak sights. Wilson Combat of course has a number of top-flight sights, with the Wilson Pyramid sight a strong favorite. In factory pistols, the choice of sights may mean moving up in price, but it will be worthwhile. If you prefer adjustable sights, and by that we mean sights that are adjustable for both windage and elevation, most makers offer that option. The main complaint concerning adjustable sights on a combat gun is that they can get knocked out of adjustment or even knocked off the gun.

A clean and neat Novak sight installation by Springfield.

During my police career, I had not only the sights, but also the hammer spur knocked off my Smith and Wesson Model 29 .44 Magnum revolver. I carried this revolver on the night I was the recipient of a blow by a two-by-four. It hit my Second Chance vest, which saved me from a severe injury, but it was not until the next day that I discovered the damage to my gun. This would not have happened with a fixed-sight revolver. I later carried a Colt Gold Cup but put it aside and returned to the Government Model after I saw the roll pin that fastened the Gold Cup's sight fail during a pistol match. Once the pin broke, the sight was launched into the air. On a professional basis I tend to be prejudiced against fully adjustable sights. New model fixed sights work just fine and allow the gun to be zeroed-in for a given load. And the adjustable sights that are currently available on the market are far tougher than anything we had in the past and are a wonderful option for the handgun experimenter. But if your 1911 is intended for use as a pure service gun and you may be serving far from home, you should opt for rugged "fixed" sights.

This ery effective half-moon or half-aperture sight from Novak is intended for short-range use.

It would be a tremendous task to do a review of the various sights available. Sights by Novak, McCormack, and Wilson are all available on factory guns. The Heinie Custom sight is among the most popular of the custom installations. While the Heinie is not a low-profile sight, it does offer a clear, sharp sight picture. One of my Action Works 1911 pistols incorporates these sights. I have come to believe that the Heinie rear sight, coupled with a Novak front post, is among the best sight combinations available. If you have a military-specification weapon or you are going full custom, these sights are an excellent option.

There are at least two middle-of-the-road options that might be considered if you are upgrading a 1911. The front sight of the 1911 is staked on and can vibrate loose. Anyone who shoots the 1911 enough may have seen this happen. King's Gunsmithing offers a set of Hardballer sights that allow the GI man to upgrade his weapon nicely. King's rear sight slides into the existing dovetail, and the front is staked on without machining. I have used several examples and they work well. Another sight is quite interesting, if not yet well proven. McCormack offers an add-on sight that is similar to its more expensive models. This sight fits the existing dovetail. A small component fits into the dovetail, and the full-size sight is screwed onto this smaller fitting. The McCormack sight gives a GI gun a racy custom look and the sight picture is greatly improved. Be aware, however, that the small GI front sight is then stuck in a lot of air because of the generous rear section of the McCormack sight. When this sight is fitted, the gun will fire high if the original front sight is retained. This is a good option that is worth exploring.

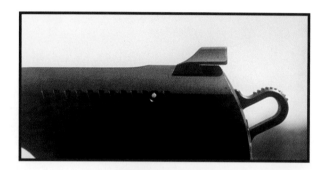

This low-mount sight is fitted by Wilson combat.

The set screw holding Novak sights steady should be checked periodically.

Night sights are never a bad option, whether they are needed or not. Night sights are iron sights that have inserts filled with radioactive tritium. The tritium gas has luminosity that is centered in a synthetic sapphire. An advantage of night sights is that they are usually mounted in high-quality iron sights. In other words, there is an improvement in the sights whether or not the night sight option is used. In dim light or darkness, the night sight glows like cat eyes. The front single dot should be green and the rear twin dots red. This contrast is a great aid in firing under conditions that do not allow for a perfect sight picture.

I have used two such sights extensively. One is the Heinie Figure Eight. A large ball is mounted in the rear sight, suspended under a smaller front ball. The other is the Wilson Combat Night Sight. I think this sight is the best factory installation, although it is installed only on top-end Wilson Combat pistols. It is a must-have on a hard-use .45. There are also various fiber-optic front sights that offer red, orange, or green fiber optics for those whose eyesight has faded. Overall, I find luminous iron sights are a good addition to the 1911 and especially worthwhile in a combat weapon.

VARIATIONS: LICENSE-BUILT, AND CLONE GUNS

43

MODEL 1911 MODEL

The military-specification 1911s built by Ithaca, Remington, and others were license-built Colts, and are not really in the spirit of this chapter. They were numerous; indeed in World War II the Remington Rand was made in greater numbers than the Colt. But the first license-built variant was the Norwegian Model of 1917. This is a difficult pistol to find but I was able to run across an example for inclusion in this work.

The Norwegian 11.25mm M1914 "1911" automatic has an extended slide release.

The Norwegian pistol is a solid 1911. When the United States improved the 1911 into the 1911A1, the Norwegians kept their pistol in 1911 form, apparently happy with the design as it was. However, the pistol did feature an enlarged slide lock and slide release, for use with gloved hands. This makes the Norwegian variant extremely interesting. The extended slide release is indeed easier to use quickly, yet it is fairly unobtrusive. The Norwegian pistol has the distinction of having been pressed into service by the Wehrmacht during the occupation of Norway in World War II. Always hungry for pistols, the Germans kept the Norwegian arsenal in production. The Norwegian pistols were discontinued after the war, but there are rumors that some were made in limited numbers in later years. The Norwegian .45 auto is quite well made, reliable, and produced of good material.

The Argentines also showed interest in the Colt pistol. The first military models in use in the pampas were Colts, but eventually manufacture was undertaken by FMAP in Argentina. The original pistols were stock

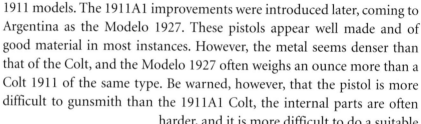

Argentina as the Modelo 1927. These pistols appear well made and of good material in most instances. However, the metal seems denser than that of the Colt, and the Modelo 1927 often weighs an ounce more than a Colt 1911 of the same type. Be warned, however, that the pistol is more difficult to gunsmith than the 1911A1 Colt, the internal parts are often

Argentina designated its 11.25mm (.45 caliber) 1911 pistol as the Colt Sistema Model 1927.

harder, and it is more difficult to do a suitable trigger job on the Modelo 1927. Just the same, they were good guns and I have had generally good results with them.

In Spain, the Llama and Star were based on the 1911 and are not true clones. The grip safeties were different, as was the profile in some respects. The Stars are much better guns than the Llamas, and the Star left the 1911 template behind. The link-and-grip safety was abandoned on the Star design and the pistol progressed to the Modelo Super, a good gun among the better examples. These pistols were most often chambered in a 9mm Largo, but some were also manufactured in .38 Supers, 9mm Lugers, and .45 ACPs.

The first attempts at producing 1911 clones were simply copies of the Colt. There have been many. The Detonics was based on the 1911; the Randall was deemed an improvement. Essex frames and slides allowed the home gunsmith to make his own 1911. These pistols are not nearly as faithful to military specifications as the military-contract pistols, and custom fitting of parts is needed. The first truly successful clone gun was the model produced by Springfield Armory. Based on castings produced in Brazil, the Springfield swept the market. Here was a

The Llama "Extra," patterned after the Colt 1911, is slightly longer than the standard 1911. The maker, Gabilondo y Cia of Elgo-ibar, Spain, has produced variants and copies of the 1911 design since 1931.

good gun with excellent fit and finish, at a price considerably lower than the Colt. Springfield continues to market military-specification weapons but also produces good examples of high-end guns.

Auto Ordnance, Para Ordnance, Rock Island Arsenal, Charles Daly, Dan Wesson, and Kimber all produce examples of 1911 clones. Even Smith and Wesson has a 1911 clone gun, with many outstanding features. Remember, some of the clones will require various levels of fitting to make them accept quality parts, and some require more fitting than others. How do the various clones stack up? We will see in the firing test section.

DO YOU NEED A CUSTOM GUN?

45

MODEL
1911
MODEL
1911
MODEL
1911
MODEL
1911
MODEL
1911
MODEL
1911
MODEL
1911
MODEL
1911
MODEL
1911
MODEL
1911
MODEL
1911
MODEL
1911
MODEL
1911
MODEL
1911
MODEL
1911
MODEL
1911
MODEL
1911
MODEL
1911
MODEL
1911
MODEL
1911
MODEL
1911
MODEL
1911

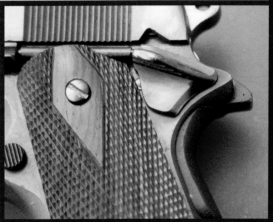

This basic Commander (top), has been modified by the addition of a custom beavertail to protect the shooter's hand and a speed safety (bottom), both provided by King's Gunworks.

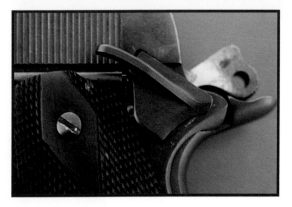

In the past many gunsmiths were able to repair broken and damaged parts and others were skilled in giving a handgun a sweet trigger or relining a barrel. But new requirements and technology have changed the way the gunsmith works. The leading beneficiaries of these changes are 1911 shooters. It was another shooter, not associated with the 1911, who spurred custom gun development. Elmer Keith pushed six-guns to their limits, occasionally pushing them too far and blowing them up. He had gunsmiths build up various frames and fit sights to his favorite revolvers, ending up with a final model, the Number Five SAA.

Service competition between the wars resulted in high-end development, and Elmer Keith's innovations proved that the handgun could be improved. Under Keith's influence, Colt 1911s were welded up and ways were found to tighten the lockup and provide accurate shots at 50 yards. The tuned guns could use target-wad-cutter ammunition. The modifications were sometimes crude while others were marvelous pieces of work, but they all worked. Anyone lucky enough to own a gun that was modified in those days owns a valuable piece of history. As time passed, however, some folks decided they wanted good sights and triggers on their 1911s, and many were so modified.

Much later, when Colonel Cooper's writings became popular, the gunsmith trade became really busy with the 1911. The bulls-eye gun gave way to the combat gun. Some pistolsmiths, unfamiliar with the needs of service shooters, simply built target guns for combat shooters. The trigger action was sometimes butchered in the attempt to make a combat gun. A too light trigger does not maintain sufficient tension with the gun's working parts and will not have a long, reliable service life. Hammers suitable for target work could be jolted off the full cock notch by recoil. Sometimes this was caught by the half cock notch, but at other times the hammer followed the slide down, resulting in a "double." A 2.5-pound bulls-eye trigger is not suitable for personal defense use. But Swenson, Clark, Pachmayr and Kings Gun Works soon learned what combat shooters needed and turned out very effective combat weapons.

The Colt factory also improved its design and production methods, and the Colt Series 70 featured a general tightening of the frame and slide and a new collet bushing that tightened the slide and barrel fit. This Series 70 was a high-water mark of Colt production. With the introduction of the Series 80, Colt also produced an Enhanced Model. This pistol featured a larger beavertail, but not something that would frighten Wilson. The safety was a little larger and the pistol now had acceptable sights. A notch under the trigger guard gave the Enhanced Models an even lower bore axis. The Series 80 pistol is usually reliable with a variety of hollow-point bullets. The sights are not Novaks but they work well enough.

Most Series 80 pistols give excellent results. The triggers are OK and the chamber-to-ramp fit is good, if not in the same class as those with a mirror-smooth polish. When deciding which of these guns to purchase as a base model for customizing and upgrades, keep one thing in mind: custom guns are a personal statement. What you wish to own is added, and nothing more. Or the sky is the limit. Grip panels, finish, and sights are yours to toy with. A Novak front and Heinie rear? No problem. A two-

This custom barrel and bushing from Storm Lake Machine in Knoxville, Tennessee, can guarantee match-grade accuracy.

The barrel on the right has a fair ramp finish, but the feed ramp on the far left has a very good custom mirror finish of the feed ramp. In the middle is a ramped barrel from Para Ordnance.

tone finish — Dane Burns can do the business. Any custom gun should demonstrate good reliability, excellent speed into action, and as much accuracy as the customer is willing to pay for. Most custom makers offer "package guns," guns offered at a reasonable price with a fixed set of options. Sights, throating, and the all-important reliability package are included.

In custom 1911s, accuracy is enhanced by the addition of a custom fit bushing, such as the one available from King's. I have tested a number of custom pistols that will all group five shots into four inches at 50 yards, from a solid rest. This is an impressive standard. Just as impressive are the Action Works pistols that will group 5 shots into just over 1 inch at 25 yards. A counterpoint to the argument that tight fitting is counterproductive to reliability is seen in Action Works pistols. The pistol is basically "as issued," but the barrel bushing is a special match-grade unit. I have cracked regular barrel bushings after firing less than 10,000 rounds. With a tighter-fitting bushing there is less slippage and slop and there is no room for battering — the pistol keeps on shooting.

When custom work is approached, we should take a hard look at the reasons behind the work. There is no need to spend money without a real need. If we are not hitting the grip safety, the manual safety is too stiff, or the gun does not feed hollow-points, then we need to contact a reputable gunsmith. Otherwise, perhaps we should leave well enough alone until we come to understand what we really need.

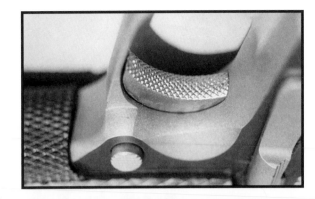

TOP:
This 1911 has been modified by the replacement of a long trigger with a short serrated version.

BOTTOM:
A popular custom addition — a long aluminum trigger.

These superb slide serrations were added by master gunsmith Bob Cogan, of Accurate Plating and weaponry.

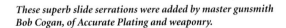

Very nice custom fit of a beavertail to a 1911 grip frame by Accurate Plating and Weaponry.

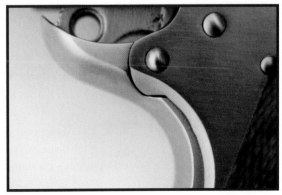

MODEL
1911
MODEL
1911
MODEL
1911
MODEL
1911
MODEL
1911
MODEL
1911
MODEL
1911
MODEL
1911
MODEL
1911
MODEL
1911
MODEL
1911
MODEL
1911
MODEL
1911
MODEL
1911
MODEL
1911
MODEL
1911
MODEL
1911
MODEL
1911
MODEL
1911
MODEL
1911
MODEL
1911
MODEL
1911
MODEL
1911
MODEL
1911
MODEL
1911
MODEL
1911
MODEL

FACTORY HIGH-GRADE CUSTOM GUNS

This chapter calls for establishing a definition of high-grade production pistols. Over the years, several gunsmiths have come to understand what most customers want in a combat gun and offer production pistols to suit those needs. By production, I mean firearms made on a factory or shop assembly line of some sort, producing a line of identical pistols. With one exception, these shops have a limited production capacity, turning out only about as many guns in one year as Colt makes in a week. Among the factory custom gun manufacturers are Wilson Combat, Ed Brown, and Les Baer. Les Baer guns, for example, have a reputation for tightness, and sometimes require a more extensive break-in than others. I have seen several in use in pistol matches. What we are discussing are individual handguns, and I really wish to cover the idea of a factory custom gun, but it is difficult to do so

The Wilson Combat Close Quarters Battle is among the most outstanding versions of the 1911 ever produced.

without discussing these examples of topflight 1911s. What Baer and others offer are loaded 1911s with full-blown custom work, but on a package basis at an affordable price. By affordable, I mean perhaps $2,000 instead of $3,000 – $4,000.

I have had extensive experience with Wilson Combat guns and they have impressed me a great deal. I have never had any kind of problem with a Wilson Combat CQB or comparable model. Nor has anyone I know — and someone would tell me! Usually shooters quietly enjoy a good pistol but shout to the hills about a bad one, especially one they paid over $1,500 for. The Wilson Combat pistols are in wide use, with excellent reputations. They offer a combination of a good trigger, excellent sights, good feed-ramp polish, a match-grade barrel, custom-grade safety and grip safety, and even beveled magazine wells, or, in some cases, a special magazine funnel. They are good buys, all things considered.

The excellent "fit and finish" of the Wilson Close Quarters Battle includes a beavertail safety.

Kimber, the single largest maker of 1911 pistols, also offers a production custom pistol. The pistol is a good one, and a main reason for Kimber's tremendous success. The workmanship is good. The triggers are usually clean and crisp, the guns feed any type of wide-mouth hollow-point, the controls are custom grade and of a good tactical design, and the sights are good. This is for Kimber's basic gun, and I find it an excellent firearm for the price. My general shooting battery includes a Kimber pistol.

The High Standard G Man is another example of a high-grade production 1911. I have no idea how many are made yearly, but production is probably limited. The pistol is a round-top-slide 1911 in general appearance. The G Man features a super-slick trigger action, black Teflon-based finish, match-grade barrel and night sights. The last time I looked it listed for just under $1,300. This is a good gun, put together by makers who know how to mas-

This Springfield Loaded Model, a factory-made 1911, features Novak adjustable sights, forward slide serrations, an extended safety, and a beavertail.

sage a 1911. I have fired mine extensively and carried it often. I can simply find no flaws with this pistol, and the appearance is more to my liking.

I have had less experience with Springfield Armory's Bureau Model. It retails for well over $1,800 and is in the Wilson and Ed Brown category. This pistol has an impeccable pedigree, having been selected by the FBI as their HRT/SWAT pistol. By all accounts it is a wonderful pistol in every way. Springfield offers a middle-of-the-road 1911, their Loaded Model, that is, in some ways, a top-end production pistol but not in the same league as the Bureau Model. I have seen examples for sale in the $500 – $700 range. The pistols have a good combination of extended safety, beavertail safety, Novak sights, and other amenities. Many of these pistols are fitted with front-slide serrations. I have owned four or five and fired close to a dozen. They are capable handguns. In one example, I raised the bar considerably by converting it as close as possible to Bureau Model standards. These pistols have given good results, and are worth the money, but they are not the performers the CQB pistol is, and they shouldn't be for the price.

I think that all of us want to own a custom handgun at some point or another. After all, a distinctive 1911, a true custom pistol, is a statement of our love for the breed. But we might ask, What will we shoot while the gun is being built? Or we may even ask, Where will the funds come from? The high-grade factory 1911 pistols are not inexpensive but they are readily available and perform very well indeed. I hope I have outlined the definition or the idea behind these pistols. The rest is up to you.

A comparison of the frame of a Wilson 1911 (bottom) with a basic model. The Wilson guns are very well made in every respect.

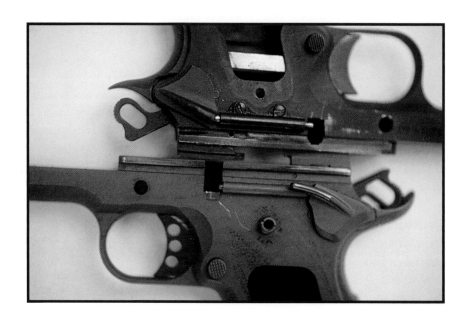

51

MODEL
1911
MODEL
1911
MODEL
1911
MODEL
1911
MODEL
1911
MODEL
1911
MODEL
1911
MODEL
1911
MODEL
1911
MODEL
1911
MODEL
1911
MODEL
1911
MODEL
1911
MODEL
1911
MODEL
1911
MODEL
1911
MODEL
1911
MODEL
1911
MODEL
1911
MODEL
1911
MODEL
1911
MODEL
1911
MODEL
1911
MODEL
1911
MODEL
1911
MODEL
1911
MODEL
1911
MODEL
1911
MODEL

LIGHTS, CAMERA, ACTION!

After the discussion of custom 1911s, it occurred to me that one section of the book should be devoted to custom shops, in order to give the reader a broader understanding of what they do. I am not saying Don Williams is the best pistolsmith in America and he would take offense at such a statement. There are a number of good gunsmiths, and several have excellent reputations. But Don's work fits my personal criteria for a top-notch carry pistol, which is, after all, what it is all about. The Action Works motto is, "Serious Guns for Serious Times." Tactics, marksmanship, and security plans count for the most, but these pistols give you an important edge as well. Some weapons have more sizzle than steak, but the Action Works guns deliver.

This well-turned-out 1911 is a product of custom gunsmith Don Williams' Arizona-based Action Works shop.

One of my 1911s has received a smooth-out package. The sharp edges have been polished or deburred. The gun was inspected and the ejector and extractor tuned as part of the reliability tune-up. The feed ramp was polished to a mirror-smooth burnish. The magazines were checked for bent feed lips. (Always send magazines with the pistol.) The action job is the most critical part of the overhaul. The action must be tuned properly or the tune-up will not last, and the trigger job will degrade and can fold under the pounding of service ammunition. In addition, any parts that are found to be too soft or too hard are discarded in the custom shop. To paraphrase Don Williams, "Some 1911s have internal parts so rough they appear to have been beat out on a rock in Pakistan!"

My preference in trigger compression on a carry gun is right at four pounds, smooth. Both of my .45s tuned by Action Works break right at this standard and have never followed or malfunctioned in firing thousands of rounds of ammunition. Details are what count. It achieves little to polish the hammer and sear contacts if the safety is not polished as well. The safety rides against the hammer, locking the hammer in place. A rough safety could scar the hammer, and there are plenty of rough aftermarket safeties. Attention to detail gives us a capable, long-lived weapon.

This custom beavertail safety has been carefully hand-fitted.

This 1911 is a very fine example of true custom work — painstaking workmanship well worth the price.

Let's take a look at one of the better pistols turned out by Action Works. First, we find high-visibility sights — a must-have. The rear sight is from Heinie, the front post a Novak. This is not a mismatch but a professional match for an optimum sight picture. A match-grade barrel bushing is also fitted. But this fit does not preclude field-stripping with the fingers. That is a neat trick, but the accuracy gain is there. The front strap of the grip frame is hand-stippled for the best purchase. Not-so-sharp, the gun abrades the hand, but you can hold onto the piece well in rapid fire, even with sweaty palms. The trigger is a dream. An accomplished handgunner may be able to wrestle a heavy trigger when firing from a bench rest, but in offhand shooting a heavy trigger is a real challenge. If firing from less than a perfect balance, a good trigger action is a great boon. The Action Works trigger allows the shooter to make the most of the weapon's intrinsic accuracy. There is no creep or backlash in the trigger.

Don can also fabricate parts. He does a really mean drop safety. The safety is lowered, with the shelf placed lower on the safety bar for slightly more rapid manipulation. This is a worthwhile modification, one that grows on you after a time. The Smith & Alexander beavertail safety is not a drop-in unit; it has to be carefully fitted. This grip safety overcomes the objection to the grip safety of the 1911. It is fast to hit, and does not require extensive effort to learn. The beavertail funnels your hand into the grip and you are ready to fire immediately. The stub on the bottom of this unit guarantees perfect hand placement.

The magazine well is beveled, a small thing but much appreciated in overall handling. Don is also an expert on handgun grips and he fitted this pistol with Ahrends custom stocks. They are not only

well checkered but relieved to clear the magazine release for a quick dump of the magazine. Rounding out the work is the attractive bead blast and matte polish combination of this stainless steel pistol. Stainless can be attractive with the proper finish, and this is it!

The pistol also features a full-length guide rod, a feature some disdain. Well, while the pistol is very much a sum of all of the work done, it does shoot better than ever with this guide rod so it will stay in the pistol! I will continue this report in the firing test session. Don also does Browning High Power pistols and the Smith and Wesson revolver, but we are interested in the 1911. This is truly a serious gun. If you are looking for your first gun, Don can take you down the right path. If you are a jaded professional, you will not be disappointed with the pistols that emerge from this shop.

This blue-steel custom 1911 is from the Action Work shop.

CAN YOU WEAR OUT A 1911?

I cling to proven designs that have stood the test of time. The Colt 1911, the Colt Single Action Army, and the Smith and Wesson Combat Magnum are among these. The CZ 75 has also earned a clean bill of health after 30 years of good service. I honestly cannot say how long the current crop of combat pistols will last, but I have educated guesses on the subject. Many are feed-reliable and reasonably well made, but time will tell. A frequent question year to year is: "How long will my 1911 last?" Guns are more often destroyed by neglect or cataclysmic abuse than by wear. Few of us would run a car without oil, but failure to lubricate the pistol is a contributing factor to many problems. By the same token, a car needs spring replacement from time to time and so does a pistol. For those who pay attention, the gun tells you when it needs springs. It will begin spitting cases farther to the rear and with more violence. The slide velocity will increase, sometimes outstripping the ability of the magazine to feed, resulting in malfunctions. Few of us keep a handgun long enough to run across these malfunctions, trading instead for the dream gun of the moment.

I have taken a hard look at the various broken handguns that I have examined and come up with the main areas of concern in a weapon's life. The foremost concern is the initial quality of the piece. After that, it's maintenance and, finally, the frequency of shooting and the pressure level

These two special .45-caliber Colts are both produced by Dane Burns of Burns Custom Pistols in Issaquah, Washington.

of the rounds used. I think maintenance is more important, and the number of rounds fired less important. The pressure of the rounds used is a consideration. We simply don't need to fire full-power loads at all times, and +P loads are best reserved for special situations. Stretching of metal parts can result from over-pressure rounds. I don't slam the slide down on an empty chamber and I am careful in manipulation of the controls. This guarantees long life and a reliable handgun. It has been argued that a custom

Master gunsmith Teddy Jacobsen of Actions by T at his workbench.

handgun with well-fitted parts will last longer than a stock gun. This is partly due to the quality of parts that may be installed, but also due to the close fitting. There is no slop in the action, no unnecessary wear. It is eccentric wear that wrecks guns; normal wear is predictable and can be dealt with by normal spring changes and replacement of high-wear parts.

The only gauge I have of how long a 1911 will last is my experience with one of the first custom 1911 pistols I owned. Teddy Jacobsen of Actions by T performed the work on a rather well worn old Series 70. It had been hard-chromed by Checkmate refinishers and worked well enough. It would not feed hollow-points and the trigger was heavy. Teddy has been called the Cops' Pistolsmith, largely due to his emphasis on action work and reliability. He does not do sight work and heavy machine work. His forte is action work, and arguably he is a master.

The Colt was a good example of his work. He delivered the pistol with a smooth four-pound trigger action, enameled the sights, and polished the feed ramp to a mirror polish. I tested the trigger by pressing my finger against the trigger and watching not the trigger but my finger. There was no movement after I felt trigger engagement — no creep at all. Sometimes, we lose trigger engagement when we have a custom trigger done. This is not good. In a few thousand rounds, the action will fail in some way. A competitor realizes that parts replacement is sometimes needed.

A cop will pay his money one time and that is all. I had not kept track of the rounds fired in this used 1911, but I probably had fired 2,000 – 3,000 rounds before Teddy's work. This was my do-everything gun, and I carried it on duty and shot competition with it. I also worked up several hot bowling pin loads, using cast-lead SWC bullets of 225 grains loaded to some 900 fps.

I had begun my writing career and was put in contact with a lawman in Alaska who carried a 1911. He did not want to carry hardball, but needed a load that would penetrate the heavy clothing worn by felons (and everyone else) in Alaska. He also felt that if need be, he would not want to feel helpless against a bear. This was about the same time a story hit of a man who defended himself against a bear with a .44 Magnum. The hollow-points all opened in the bear's tough outer hide and failed to adequately penetrate!

This was before the 230-grain Hornady XTP, but we did have the 250-grain XTP, designed for the .45 Colt. I used heavy springs and a Wilson shock buffer and worked up a load that was hot as a depot stove —

250 grains at 930 fps or so. The 255-grain-cast SWC, which I preferred, would do about 15 fps more. The XTP expanded to a degree and certainly gave adequate penetration. A custom loader supplied quite a few to this man. I fired perhaps 500 or more in working the load up and decided to use it in my bowling pin matches. I won several using this load.

Now we get to the point. I carefully kept tabulations of the rounds fired in the Jacobsen Colt. About 50 percent of the rounds fired were hardball or the equivalent, usually a 230-grain cat bullet over enough Bullseye to do 850 fps. The rest were just a little hotter, either the loads I carried on duty or the bowling pin loads. And a good number were much hotter, the "pin" loads. I used W.C. Wolff premium springs, as originally installed by Teddy. Here are the results:

At 11,500 rounds the barrel bushing cracked. I replaced it with a King's match version. The gun did not stop firing when the bushing broke, but the original Colett bushing was cracked. The finger fell off when I broke the gun down. At 13,700 rounds the slide stop broke. The gun did not tie up but it would not stop the slide when the magazine was empty. I replaced the unit with a Wilson Combat slide stop — in blue! At 14,500 rounds the plunger tube came apart and I had to have it staked back on. Finally, at 15,750 rounds the frame cracked, just in front of the trigger guard, and the gun still worked.

This is a lot of ammunition, and frankly most of it was much hotter than anything I would use today. What I did was equivalent to running the family sedan at 100 miles per hour nonstop every other day for 100,000 miles. The work Teddy did never failed. The trigger action smoothed a little with use, but the gun never failed to fire or doubled. The grip safety engagement remained just as Teddy specified, and it never failed. The gun fed, chambered, and fired everything I fed it. So here we have a well-worn

DANE BURNS' 1911 RELIABILITY PACKAGE

If you want your 1911 to be a reliable friend, I recommend a few modifications that will prove beneficial in the long run. This reliability package is offered by Dane Burns, Actions by T, or the Action Works. I highly recommend this simple procedure. As Dane Burns tells us the reliability package is a bargain compared, with doing each thing at one time. He has the gun in hand and can make everything all right at once.

- Adjust and polish extractor.
- Install premium recoil and firing pin springs and shock buff.
- Throat barrel and polish feed ramp.
- Check fit of sear and disconnector.
- Function-test safeties.

1911 that fired almost 20,000 rounds with minimal parts breakage. And the trigger action was still fine! I sold this gun to a friend who wished to own it as a home defense gun. The crack in the frame? A lot of 1911s get those. The gun still works. But this friend has fired perhaps 500 rounds in this gun in five years. He has a very good gun.

FBI tests and my own experience confirm that a 1911 will go 20,000 rounds and remain in good condition, well suited for self-defense. That is more than most of us will fire in a lifetime in a single pistol, but less than serious competitors might fire in three years.

The author fires one of his 1911s during a target session. The 1911 design is tough and reliable — capable of giving a life-time of service.

HANDGUN FINISHES

There are many finishes available for handguns. Some represent vanity on the part of the owner, while others answer a real need. No one finish is perfect for every situation, but some are well suited to the individual's needs. Much is made of a non-reflective surface. This is vital in military terms, but in civilian situations a bright finish is quite acceptable. More than a few old-time officers felt that a bright, reflective finish lent an extra caliber to a handgun, making it appear larger! The primary duty of the finish is protection from corrosion.

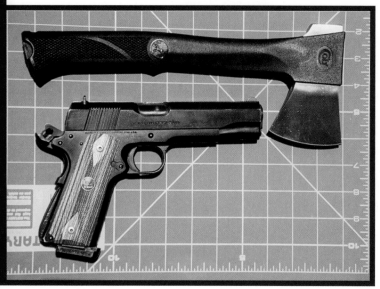

This 1911A1-type Colt, shown here with a Colt survival ax, is finished in space-age Bear Coat, a Teflon coating from Rocky Mountain Arms .

A pistol in the white, one without any type of finish, would rust quite quickly. Bluing is the traditional answer. Bluing is the king of controlled rust. I admit I find bluing very attractive and it does serve well if properly done. But all finishes are not made for the type of work I put a handgun to. As a young officer on special assignment, I often carried a handgun very close to my body. The strong salts in perspiration quickly attacked the finish, and not only the outer surface, but the inner workings of the pistol as well. I realized something more was needed. I was also engaged in a practice that may not have been foreseen by the manufacturer. I engaged in a daily habit of presenting my weapon from the holster. A dozen or so draws a day from a tightly fitted holster is a minimum standard for real proficiency, and this practice paid off well. It also quickly wore away parts of the gun's conventional finish. I have tested practically every type of finish since those early days, and came away with a good understanding of each. But first you must understand your needs. Some finishes are very hard and resist wear, others fight corrosion, and others eliminate the need for lubrication.

Blue remains a popular finish, but you will find few genuine highly polished blued-steel pistols on the market. Most commercial pistols have a

This Commander features a hard chrome finish from Accurate Plating and Weaponry.

kind of inexpensive blue called matte finish. These pistols will wear more quickly than those with a standard blued finish, because matte is rougher than polished blue and will abrade in the holster more quickly. A good choice seldom seen today is Parkerizing, a phosphate etching process. Used extensively on military weapons, beginning just before World War II, Parkerizing is a pretty decent low-maintenance finish.

I still believe that one of the best choices is stainless steel. Just as aluminum frames were the innovation of the 1950s, stainless steel was the coming thing in the 1960s. Stainless steel is just that — "stain less." It will rust and is far more resistant to corrosion than carbon steel. Early stainless guns were sometimes subject to galling, but this was solved by subtle changes in the makeup of the metal alloy used. When Colt introduced its stainless steel Government Model, it was quickly hailed as the most reliable of all modern Colts. This is a strong statement, but for some reason the stainless Colts seem to have better triggers, feed hollow-points better, and are even more accurate than blue-steel Colts. The only explanation I have is that stainless is a bit harder to work than carbon steel so the extra care in manufacture paid off!

Stainless will solve corrosion problems better, given regular maintenance. Special care must be given in lubrication in some cases, but not in others. Let your individual pistol be your guide. I have used one stainless pistol extensively that simply would not work unless lubricated, but when properly lubed fired anything. Factory stainless is sometimes rough in appearance but it can be bead blasted and made quite attractive. Action Works has done this for me on several occasions, with good results.

The hardest finish available is hard chrome. When done properly, a hard-chromed gun will be highly resistant to wear. I literally broke and wore out a holster practicing with my hard-chromed Accurate Plating

Commander, but never noted any perceptible wear to the finish. Hard chrome will pick up rust if it is not wiped clean occasionally, but the spots really jump out at you on the chrome surface and are easily wiped away. Stainless is nowhere near as resistant to corrosion as hard chrome. This finish does build up tolerance, however, and the man or woman who applies hard chrome must know what he or she is doing. If you are having custom work done, have it done before the plating process or discuss the finish with your gunsmith before doing a custom workup. Hard chrome is a good finish and a good show finish if you are working up a pistol to impress your friends. There is nothing wrong with that; I have seen a number of guns that were both beautiful as well as functional.

I have also used an NP 3 plated handgun finished by Robar Custom Metal Finishing of Phoenix, Arizona, with good results. This finish combines electroless nickel with Teflon (polytetrafluorothylene). This Teflon is a high-tech version of the stuff frying pans are coated with and it works well. The Teflon component means the finish requires less lubrication than some finishes, but it will definitely require some lubrication. Robar also offers a number of other finishes I am less familiar with, but my overall contact with the company has been good.

I have also fired, carried, and tested pistols that have the highly developed Bearcoat finish produced by Colorado-based Rocky Mountain Arms. Bearcoat is DuPont Teflon combined with epoxy and melamine resin. This finish is offered in several colors, including camouflage. It is self-lubricating — oil it and the lubricant will simply run off — and highly corrosion resistant, but not as wear resistant as some. Still, thousands of presentations from the holster and several hard knocks gave me a good idea of the efficiency of this finish.

TOP:
This stainless steel Colt is a practical, workmanlike everyday performer.

BOTTOM:
This High Standard G Man came from the factory with a high-tech Teflon finish.

Overall, after a hard look I find that Bearcoat is best suited to my needs over any other finish. It protects the weapon and eliminates any need for lubrication — although the gun still needs to be cleaned. Bearcoat sheds unburned powder readily in cleaning. Oil and solvent do not gum up the action and solvent residue seems to be repelled once the job is done. I once had to fire a Bearcoat-finished firearm during a critical incident. The pistol came out of a mud-soaked holster and fired — and cycled — normally. That gives you a lot of confidence in this type of handgun finish.

The type of finish on your 1911 can be a very important decision. Choose well: the life of the firearm and perhaps of the user depend upon it.

THE .45 ACP CARTRIDGE

61

MODEL
1911
MODEL
1911
MODEL
1911
MODEL
1911
MODEL
1911
MODEL
1911
MODEL
1911
MODEL
1911
MODEL
1911
MODEL
1911
MODEL
1911
MODEL
1911
MODEL
1911
MODEL
1911
MODEL
1911
MODEL
1911
MODEL
1911
MODEL
1911
MODEL
1911
MODEL
1911
MODEL
1911
MODEL
1911
MODEL
1911
MODEL
1911

It is my contention that the .45 Automatic Colt Pistol cartridge is the most efficient anti-personnel round that we are ever likely to produce. My conclusions are based upon hard fact, historical evidence, and laboratory results. I do not make claims to any secret knowledge, and I don't use statistics. As a young student in the lab, and as a peace officer called upon to testify in court, I was reminded that my findings had to be verifiable. To be valid, an experiment must be repeatable. Colonel Cooper argued that statistics are often used by rascals to impress fools. The facts presented will stand until, to paraphrase writer Chuck Taylor, the basic laws of physics are changed.

Before and after: Speer Gold Dot bullets as used in Black Hills 230 -grain jacketed hollow-point loads.

The .45 ACP offers a balance of power, controllability, penetration, and, given proper bullets, expansion. This balance is not a delicate one. One or more of the components can be compromised and the cartridge still works well. A light bullet can be used as well as a bullet of low velocity and the cartridge will still perform well. The .45 relies on frontal area and mass to do its work. While it does not require expansion to be effective, expansion is desirable if we can attain it. The .45 ACP also is very efficient in burning powder. Many differing loads will show a full powder burn. The benefits of the .45 auto are not immediately obvious. The .45 ACP is, first of all, a combat cartridge, but it is also a practical all-around cartridge. The .45 Colt and .45 Auto Rim (both revolver cartridges) are similar in performance and versatility to the .45 ACP and in fact are more powerful, but both must be hand-loaded for truly good performance.

The .45 ACP was developed from the classic .45 Colt. The .45 Colt performed well at relatively long range against aboriginal tribesmen and horses and the round could drop a war pony as well as a hardened plains warrior. Army Chief of Ordnance Steven Benet specified a .45-caliber center-fire cartridge for the 1873 Colt service revolver, and the .45 Colt was

The author holds an expanded Winchester SXT.

the result. When the .45 ACP was in embryonic form, there was some experimentation with case length and extractor groove diameter. The semi-rim that plagued the .38 ACP was eliminated in the .45. Here was a true, modern, smokeless-powder, rimless semiauto cartridge. Designer John Browning once believed that 1,000 fps was needed to guarantee successful auto pistol performance, and, at the time, there was some evidence to support his belief. Early loadings of the .45 ACP used a 200-grain bullet at 1,000 fps. (Among the most accurate service loads I have tested are custom loads from Mastercast, where a 200-grain Hornady XTP is jolted to 992 fps.) But the Army demanded a heavier bullet and, in the end, a 230-grain bullet at 850 fps was chosen. No other semiauto cartridge of this diameter and power saw a fraction of the use the .45 ACP did. (The British .455 Webley automatic was certainly a good cartridge, but was produced in insignificant numbers.)

ABOVE:
These high velocity JHPs give fine expansion.

ABOVE RIGHT:
The Cor-Bon JHP always gives good expansion, especially at short range.

The .45 ACP is powerful but comfortable to fire in a well-designed handgun. The small propellant charge in the .45 ACP burns quickly and efficiently, producing little muzzle flash and recoil energy. The .45 exhibits a full burn in most cases, which means it burns the complete powder charge inside the barrel, and its accuracy and consistency are enhanced. Some cartridges are noted for producing extreme balls of fire in dim light. This muzzle flash can temporarily blind the shooter. Magnum pistol cartridges are considerable offenders. These cartridges operate in what is called an over-bore condition. Chamber erosion or top-strap cutting are common. A method of testing for this condition is simple and shows the efficiency of the .45. Place a white target at perhaps three yard's distance from the muzzle of your handgun. Fire a round into the center. At this range most calibers will speckle the target with unburned powder, but not the .45.

The .45 ACP operates at low pressure. The standard operating pressure is 18,000 pounds per square inch (psi). The .45 Colt can push a 250-grain bullet to 800 fps with only 12,000 psi. On the other hand, the .45 ACP achieves 18,000 psi to push 230 grains to 850 fps. The 9mm Luger, .40-caliber Smith & Wesson, and .357 SIG operate in the 30,000 psi range. I won't fall into the trap of comparison; I will let the .45 ACP stand on its own merit. By any measure, it is an efficient cartridge.

The .451-inch, 230-grain bullet is relatively long for a handgun bullet and is well balanced. The .45 ACP load can give up some bullet weight and retain a long-bearing surface, which is important to accuracy potential. A 200-grain semi-wad-cutter (SWC) bullet has nearly the same bearing surface as a 230-grain bullet. Bullet weights of 152 to 260 grains produce good accuracy and sufficient energy to perform a variety of tasks. A considerable argument can be made for expanding bullets in the .45 ACP, but flat-point and even heavy hardball or round-nose configurations in this caliber have proven effective for personal defense.

Hardball or military full-metal-jacketed .45-caliber ammunition has a tremendous reputation, which some have chosen to dismiss as mere legend or tall tales. The .45 military round has a well-proven record. Still, that modern expanding bullets can be even more effective should be obvious. I have collected shooting histories for many years. My reports began with newspaper reports and court reports. When a peace officer says he has seen the effect of a certain caliber, he means he arrived just as the fight was over. I have seen my share, and few handgun calibers are impressive. My observations indicate that the small calibers, from .25 ACP to the non-expanding .38s, are all about the same in effectiveness. A study carried out by the Police Marksman's Association (PMA) reached the same conclusions. Study director, Dick Fairburn found that .38 and 9mm caliber, non-expanding bullets could put down a felon on average about one time in four, with a single shot fired. In popular parlance, that is 25 percent effective. Hardball .45s performed at about 60 percent.

When driven to sufficient velocity, even heavy .45 hollow-points expand or fragment. This is from a +P load fired in a six-inch barrel "long slide" gun.

The prudent man realizes that differences in size, muscle, motivation, and level of intoxication must be taken into account. Many street drugs started out as painkillers. These drugs were designed to suppress pain, and they do the job as intended, making it difficult to count upon pain compliance as a method of stopping violent action. Motivated, toughened hoodlums can be difficult to stop with handgun bullets. Leave behind the myth of the spacedout junkie; street thugs are hardened by their lifestyle. Many have spent time in penitentiaries, where you cannot make it without well-developed survival skills.

From left to right, the 9mm, .40 and .45. By any criterion, physics favors the bigger bullet.

In .45 ammunition, feed reliability and quality come first. These Triton loads passed our stringent test program.

The .45 ACP does not rely upon any one special loading, a variety give good performance. The 9mm Luger, as a comparison, can run a 100 percent deviation in penetration between loadings. The .45 ACP performs in a narrower spectrum. While none of the .45 loadings are a poleax or Thor's hammer, but they are well balanced and effective within the limits of a handgun cartridge. The argument is often made that small caliber weapons are easier to control. The PMA study put a lie to that precept. Officers trained in the use of the .45 ACP and the .357 Magnum were normally trained to a higher standard. They produced more hits per shots fired than officers armed with lighter weapons. Those carrying a weapon with poor wound ballistics and poor hit probability are ill armed indeed.

A point in favor of the .45 is made in the 1960 edition of the *Handgunner's Guide* written by Chic Gaylord. Gaylord worked closely with the New York police and debriefed quite a few gunfight survivors. He felt that several .38 loads might not immediately put a man down, but usually proved fatal if delivered in batches of four to six rounds in the body. On the other hand, Gaylord determined that a single .45 in the shoulder would usually stop a man even if it did not generally prove fatal — a learned opinion that makes much sense today. It is incumbent upon all who choose a defensive handgun cartridge to consider all the evidence and to disregard unverifiable reports and unrepeatable testing. To base procedure on bankrupt methodology is bad policy.

The availability of modern expanding bullets have increased the effectiveness of many cartridges, especially in medium bore sizes. Arguably the mid-bores were most in need of help. Small bores, such as the .32 ACP, need penetration to guarantee any hope of effectiveness, and expanding bullets negate this penetration. The mid bores, the .38 Special and the 9mm Luger, make good use of hollow-point bullets. Bu the fact remains that the .45 will make good to excellent use of any of a wide range of expanding bullets.

An attribute of the .45 that cannot be overstated is accuracy. The .45 was first used in competition simply because it was the service cartridge, but gunsmiths learned that the 1911 could be modified tightened and tweaked into an accurate combination. The most accurate handgun is useless without a good cartridge. The .45 ACP, simply, is as accurate as any handgun cartridge.

SERVICE AMMUNITION

I have had the opportunity to perform a comprehensive test of a wide spectrum of defense and service ammunition. This test has altered my preferences and may alter your perceptions. The performance of these cartridges, in the main, has proven consistent and excellent. The quality of American ammunition production is the best it has ever been and is steadily improving. The need for improved ballistics has been fully met by the American firearms and ammunition establishment.

Handguns are not very powerful by nature and what power they have must be harnessed as efficiently as possible. Any service load must have adequate penetration. Light cover, car glass, and heavy clothing can prove to be a daunting barrier. A significant number of police

We fired this group in rapid fire at 25 yards with Fiocchi ammunition, then moved to 50 yards and fired the second group off-hand, with a Kimber Custom II.

shootings involve felons in vehicles. This demands a cartridge with good penetration. Some have stated that I put too much emphasis on penetration. I have seen a 200-grain, .45-caliber hollow-point that came apart upon striking a car windshield. The jacket was embedded in the glass and the core had fallen spent in the front seat. This is not the type of performance I want. When you are facing an adversary, he may well be firing at you or otherwise threatening you. His arms may be outstretched toward you, perhaps holding a weapon. The bullet you fire at him must penetrate the heavy arm bones if need be, in addition to any heavy clothing he may be wearing, and continue to drive deep enough to reach the blood-bearing organs. Do you really want to carry a load that is on the low side in penetration?

The author has enjoyed excellent luck with Western powders.

RELIABLE AND ACCURATE HANDGUN AMMUNITION

What follows are the results of a test of some of the more effective handgun ammunition currently available. These loads have proven reliable and accurate, and should meet your needs.

COMMERCIAL AMMUNITION

Loading	Velocity	Penetration	Expansion
Triton 165-grain Quik Shok*	1,199 fps	10.0	4.2 dispersion
Cor Bon 165-grain JHP	1,231 fps	9.6	.55 F
Speer 185-grain Gold Dot	999 fps	14.9	.60
Remington 185-grain JHP	1,004 fps	9.5	.88
Remington 185-grain JHP+P	1,149 fps	10.5	.90
Winchester Silvertip	971 fps	11.0	.78
Cor Bon 200-grain JHP	1,076 fps	10.9	.69 F
Mastercast 200-grain JHP	992 fps	14.0	.68
Wilson Combat 200-grain JHP	1,005 fps	13.8	.69
Speer 200-grain Gold Dot +P	1,066 fps	12.0	.75
Hornady 200-grain XTP	1,071 fps	14.5	.69
Federal Hydra Shock 230-grain JHP	870 fps	13.8	.72
Federal TACTICAL**	848 fps	16.0	.66
Winchester 230-grain SXT	866 fps	14.5	.70
Winchester 230-grain SXT +P	911 fps	13.0	.78
Cor-Bon 230-grain JHP	919 fps	12.0	.78
Speer Gold Dot	860 fps	14.2	.74
PMC Starfire	862 fps	14.0	.69
Black Hills 230-grain JHP	898 fps	13.5	.76
Black Hills 230-grain JHP +P	952 fps	15.0	.70
Remington 230-grain Golden Saber	872 fps	15.0	.69
Hornady 230-grain JHP +P	922 fps	15.5	.68

HANDLOADS

Hornady 250-grain XTP	909 fps	16.9	.52
Northwest Custom Projectile 300-grain JSP	867 fps	26.5	.48

Penetration and expansion are expressed in inches.

F = fragmented into pieces.

*The three equal parts of the bullet are designed to disperse in the target.

**This is a load with a bonded core that offers higher penetration, designed especially for police use.

It is noteworthy that some loads, despite using the same bullet, such as the XTP and the Gold Dot, showed different performance due to a slight deviation in velocity.

HANDLOADING THE .45 ACP

If you are going to practice regularly with a 1911 and are not independently wealthy, then you must handload. Handloading is less complicated than operating a ham radio and less dangerous than using a jackhammer, but the rules must be respected. A good loading manual is a primary prerequisite, and a little common sense goes a long way. The steps in handloading a centerfire cartridge are carefully outlined in your loading manual, and too extensive to cover in full. Remember, concentration upon the task at hand is demanded. You can blow a gun up and you can get hurt if you are careless, so be alert at all times.

A single-stage press is best for beginners, and more than acceptable for working up precision.

Because the .45 ACP is a straight-walled cartridge, it is easier to handload than a bottlenecked rifle cartridge. It is also easier to deal with than Magnum cartridges and bottleneck or semibottlenecks such as the .357 SIG and .44-40. The .45 is, in fact, a joy to load — an efficient cartridge that seems to do well with most powder and bullet combinations. I still use the old standbys, Unique and Bullseye, but have ventured into loading with the various

Hogdon and Western powders. As for gear, I have a combination of Lee, Hornady, and RCBS loading equipment. I use single-stage presses for precision loading and graduate to turret types for high output. As a beginning system, you can't beat the RCBS Rockchucker. This big, brawny press is made of good material and is practically indestructible. If you are a high-output shooter, then you may wish to invest in a Dillon progressive loader. The Dillon is first class and the company backs the press up with an ironclad warranty. I have used an RCBS Little Dandy powder scale in working up most of the loads featured in this book, with excellent results.

These 185-grain SWC bullets are economical and accurate.

A piece of equipment you will need is a chronograph. Measuring velocity is always interesting, but a chronograph also measures the standard deviation of loads. This is the difference in velocity between rounds. Here is a sample string of rounds and their velocity variation:

1 — 800 fps
2 — 810 fps
3 — 801 fps
4 — 811 fps

The standard deviation is 10 feet per second — a very good standard. In the real world, even the best factory ammunition seldom can exhibit an

SD better than 20 fps. I have tested ammunition with a high SD of 35 fps that was quite accurate, but this is against the odds. In some shooting sports handgun ammunition must meet a certain power factor, and the only way to know this before the bullets are tested at the match is to check the velocity.

When loading my own ammunition, I have come to prefer hard-cast lead bullets. I have a two-cavity mold from Ballisti Cast that throws pretty well cut, and definitely accurate, bullets. I am never happier than when firing my own cast bullets — and I can work up .45s that cost little more than .22 rimfires by casting my own bullets from wheel weights. But I simply can't cast enough in a limited amount of time to satisfy my needs. Cast bullets provided by Leadhead, Oregon Trail, Star, Phoenix, Precision, Hunter's Supply, Rimrock, and others have given excellent results. Some of the most accurate handloads I have used have been fired with the Black Lion flat-point .45 bullet. Even the simple 200-grain RNL bullet from Leadhead has given good results.

Handloading gives the opportunity to tailor rounds to any need. You can load a 165-grain bullet at 830 fps for a beginner to initiate him or her to the 1911. You can also load a walloping 255-grain SWC for bowling pin competition that is sure to spin the pins on their tails, or you can load a Hornady XTP for deer-sized game. Or, for maximum accuracy, you may choose Sierra's 185-grain Match bullet.

These hard-cast 255-grain SWC bullets are loaded to about 900 fps for pin Competition.

LOADS FOR THE .45 ACP

At this point it would be fashionable to recommend the top loads for personal defense and hunting. If you are not a handloader, then you are limited to factory ammunition. That's not bad, since there are a number of very good loads. I have several friends who took deer with the Remington 185-grain JHP in the days before the +P variant. Most of those who have defended themselves with the .45 used hardball ammunition, without complaint. But if we can have a hollow-point, we need to use it. My recommendation for service use is the 230-grain JHP from Black Hills, Speer, Winchester, Federal, or Remington. Use the one that feeds flawlessly into your weapon and gives good accuracy. Lighter bullets are acceptable in some loadings, but traditionally the 1911 functions best with 230-grain bullets. This is especially true of the shorter-slide weapons such as the Commander. Still, the 185-grain Remington load has an excellent track record. I have also fired over a thousand rounds of Black Hills 185-grain JHP with perfect function.

One of the better gunsmiths and overall experts on the 1911 to emerge in the previous century is Bill Wilson. Wilson Combat offers what Bill believes to be a top-notch defense load for the 1911. He is not shy about listing both loads that usually feed well into the 1911 and those that give trouble. I have found nothing to disagree with in anything he has recommended. Wilson offers a custom load using the 200-grain Hornady XTP bullet. Mastercast offers much the same load. Either goes at about 1,000 fps in a five-inch barrel. Penetration is on the long side, with outstanding accuracy. This is a good load with an impressive recommendation. While I prefer 230-grain loads, there is nothing wrong with either of these 200-grain-bullet loads.

For those who cannot carry a hollow-point by rule of law or official sanction, the .45 ACP is among a very few cartridges that perform well in the personal defense role without an expanding bullet. The Hornady jacketed flat-point would be my first choice in this situation. In fact, my pistols are loaded with this ammunition on a regular basis. My guns are all-arounders, and while self-defense is the primary prerequisite, I am just as likely to get a shot at a deer or even a wild turkey. A big bullet with a flat nose has worked before and will work again.

There are various specialty loadings for the .45 that offer considerable versatility. While these loads are available in other calibers, the .45 ACP makes the most of each. Among the most useful are various frangible loads. Black Hills loads are a good example, and International Cartridge specializes in the type. The bullets are of sintered material, metal particles that have been bonded together by heat and pressure. When they strike metal, they disintegrate. This makes for safe training when steel targets are used. Even live-fire automobile assaults may be safely practiced with this type of ammunition. I have tested the International Cartridge loads extensively. They work very well, and the loads are accurate and reliable — all we can ask. They burn clean as well. For practice on steel plates, these are the best choice. I used the International Cartridge loads in a Gibson metal reactive target with excellent results.

There are many good factory loads available. The best choice is the one that feeds well into your gun and is accurate — shooting straight is most important.

A special shell for ridding the homestead of pests or vermin is the shot shell. Originally developed for inclusion in military survival packs, this allows the .45 to launch a small payload of number-nine shot. Usually, 150 to 175 pellets are included in the load. I have fired about a hundred rounds of the CCI shot shell in various .45s. The long case feeds in all guns I have tested, but since it is longer than standard-length brass, it sometimes hangs on

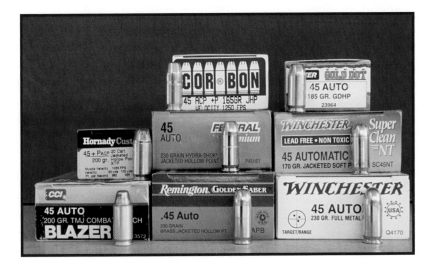

the ejection port of Colt Series 70-type pistols. But it is great sport to blast off a magazine of shot shells through my Commander. Stunts such as taking out flying balloons can be great sport. Of course, be careful and be certain there is no ball ammo to confuse the issue. The shot pattern is good enough to take out a snake, rat, or other vermin from up to about 15 feet, perhaps a little farther. Under no circumstances should any type of shot shell be considered for self-defense. Even at contact distance, penetration is not adequate, and I cannot say that the cartridges are 100 percent feed reliable. That is simply the nature of the beast. CCI Speer has done a wonderful job making shot cartridges work in most modern pistols, and they are good recreational cartridges. As for hunting or survival use, well, you would have to sneak up pretty close to a bunny with this load. I have also fired Winchester and Remington shot shells with generally similar results, but the Speer load seems to be the only one with wide distribution.

The Glaser Safety Slug was designed to provide both maximum impact and a degree of safety in a risky environment such as an airliner. The Safety Slug is built using only the jacket of a jacketed hollow-point bullet. The jacket is then filled with bird shot and the cap sealed with epoxy or a bonding agent. The theory is that the bullet, when striking a hard object, breaks up safely without dangerous overpenetration. When the bullet strikes an animate object, the bullet opens and the payload is released. The shot travels in clumps and often shreds organs. In other cases the nose can collapse and the bullet may not open at all. The Glaser bullet was originally designed for the .38 Special cartridge. It does get the .38 up off its feet. The cartridge, however, is expensive, since it is virtually handmade, making a reliability test difficult. Still, the Glaser is a legendary round that is a counterpoint to standard hollow-points. For air marshal or courtroom security work, it just may be the best choice.

The Cor-Bon Pow'R Ball was designed to address the problem of feed reliability in older 1911s. This load uses a special bullet that has a hollow point but features a ball in the hollow nose to give hardball-like feed reliability. When the bullet impacts flesh, the ball is driven back into the hollow point and the bullet expands. The PowR Ball bullet is lighter than standard, at 165 grains in the .45 ACP, and travels at perhaps 1,200 fps. Per my testing, the load feeds even into foreign-made 1911s and older military guns. It expands well in tests. The Pow'R Ball is a counterpoint to hardball, and a viable option.

In closing, we will look at the best bullets available from Winchester, Federal, Remington, Speer, and Hornady. Win-

The need to penetrate vehicle glass is often an important consideration.

chester's SXT bullet resembles the Silvertip in that it has a "crease and fold design," but performs with more penetration while retaining excellent expansion. The SXT uses a reverse-taper jacket. Winchester tells me the soft lead core is designed to move in the jacket when resistance is met. There is a deep, hollow point along with six serrations in the nose of the jacket to aid in bullet upset by weakening the bullet. The SXT offers excellent feed reliability and I have found expansion consistent.

International Cartridge frangible loads and the Gibson steel target are a good combination.

Federal's Hydra Shock is a hollow-point bullet of conventional design in most regards, with one exception. The Hydra Shock features a post in the middle of the hollow point. This post is intended to direct fluid pressure to the inside walls of the jacket, helping to instigate expansion. The Hydra Shock has seen much use in personal defense and I have viewed a number of autopsy photos showing Hydra Shock performance. This is a good bullet and proven design and is accurate enough with excellent expansion potential.

The Remington Golden Saber features a jacket made of cartridge brass instead of the standard copper jacket. The jacket is stiffer than that found on other bullets. It is not simply serrated to induce expansion, but cut completely through. When the bullet strikes an object and expands, the metal actually expands in a circular, sawing pattern. The Golden Saber was chosen by the FBI for use in HRT and SWAT pistols, and was required to meet stringent requirements. The bullet also features a driving band, a special component that lends greater bearing surface to the bullet. The jacket itself is part of the expanded diameter of this bullet.

The Hornady XTP bullet is among the most accurate handgun bullets ever produced. The XTP will be found to be on the long end in penetration, while retaining good expansion. Some bullets lose penetration when driven faster, since the bullet expands and stops more quickly. The XTP not only expands more at high velocity, it penetrates more deeply as well. For those whose needs call for more penetration, the XTP is a good choice. Notably, Bill Wilson's defense load, the only example featured by Wilson Combat, uses a 200-grain XTP. Mastercast, a respected custom loader, also uses the XTP, and the XTP is used in Texas Ammunition's .45 Super ammunition. We could go on, but rest assured that the XTP is a highly respected bullet in the professional community.

The Speer Gold Dot features a bonded core. In other words, the bullet is as much one piece as possible, with core separation unlikely at handgun velocities. The bullet core or lead component itself is fluted to achieve expansion. The bullets are consistent in performance and accuracy. Over time, the Gold Dot has turned in exceptional results. This is a bullet well worth considering for personal defense.

72

MODEL
1911
MODEL
1911
MODEL
1911
MODEL
1911
MODEL
1911
MODEL
1911
MODEL
1911
MODEL
1911
MODEL
1911
MODEL
1911
MODEL
1911
MODEL
1911
MODEL
1911
MODEL
1911
MODEL
1911
MODEL
1911
MODEL
1911
MODEL
1911
MODEL
1911
MODEL
1911
MODEL
1911
MODEL
1911

OTHER CALIBERS

After expressing my considerable respect and enthusiasm for the .45 ACP cartridge, I now must cover the alternatives. Some are good cartridges, if not as versatile as the .45 ACP. I have included the cartridges I have extensive experience with. In my opinion, the .22, .38 Super, and .45 ACP are the most practical choices for the 1911.

This pistol, fitted with a Wilson Combat .22-caliber conversion unit, is well suited for practice and practical shooting.

.22 LONG RIFLE

This is not an included here as an alternative cartridge in the manner in which the others are listed. The .22 is a companion to the .45 or practically any other caliber. The .22 can be used in 1911 pistols by installing conversion units that consist of a complete alternate slide, barrel, and magazine. These .22 conversion kits are tremendous training resources and a recreational delight. Many units, including the version offered by Wilson Combat, are accurate enough to be used for hunting small game. This is a fine sub-caliber option, well worth owning. I don't consider a 1911 complete without a rimfire conversion unit. Personal defense is a deadly serious business, but no one said we are not allowed to have fun and to enjoy recreation with handguns. The .22 Rimfire defines fun and recreation.

9MM PARABELLUM (LUGER)

There would seem to be little point in including the 9mm Luger in a 1911 format. The Super completely outpaces it and the .45 overwhelms small-bore cartridges. Still, there are those who feel that the 9mm Luger is an adequate defense cartridge and prefer the 1911, and there are overseas sales to consider. In many nations, the 9mm is the cartridge of choice and the .45 ACP is difficult to procure. I have owned a custom Commander in .38 Super that had a 9mm barrel (all the conversion paraphernalia that is normally required) included as a spare along with magazines to fire 9mm in the Super. The Commander featured a Bar Sto barrel in .38 Super. I fired all of the surplus 9mm ammunition I could find. This is one option and the one that makes the most sense, using the 9mm as an understudy for the .38 Super. The 9mm Commander in particular was a nice gun. To convert a 9mm model to .38 Super, some stretching of the extractor and perhaps opening the breech face is required. But the 9mm barrel usually works fine in the Super. Normally, stock 9mm guns are more accurate than stock .38 Super guns and recoil less than the Super or the .45.

Several calibers are chambered by the 1911 pistols — (left to right) .40-caliber Smith & Wesson, .357 SIG, .45 ACP, and .400 Cor-Bon.

Be certain to use proper magazines in the 9mm, not Supers with blocks, for the shorter round. If you use the 9mm for personal defense, two factory loadings excel in this caliber. The Texas Ammunition 115-grain load using the XTP bullet breaks a solid 1,340 fps in a five-inch Colt. The Cor-Bon load has less penetration but expands quickly, producing about the same velocity.

THE .38 SUPER

As I discussed in the section on the development of the Super .38, the Supers have excellent penetration characteristics. Loaded with Cor-Bon ammunition, it is a superb defense cartridge. A 115-grain JHP, at over 1,400 fps, has to get the bad guy's attention! I also enjoy handloading the Super. It is an efficient cartridge with many good attributes. For example, my favorite Super load pushes the 124-grain Ranier JHP to over 1,365 fps when propelled by a stiff charge of Unique. There is no unburned powder and little muzzle flash. The 9mm cannot compare to the Super when someone who knows what they are about is at the loading bench. With heavy bullets such as the 147-grain 9mm XTP, the Super can be a good performer, if you prefer heavyweights.

The .38 Super is a better choice than the .357 SIG in the 1911 format, but they are similar in performance. The Super has excellent feed reliability, particularly with modern Metalform magazines. If you have a real need for more penetration than the .45 ACP offers, the Super is a good choice. If you worship the high-velocity fragmenting-bullet totem, this is the 1911 caliber for you. Many of the comments in praise of the 9 x 23mm also apply to the Super, but the Super is not as powerful as the 9 x 23.

This is a modernized .38 Super with an ultrastrong case. The factory load propels a 125-grain Silvertip to a solid 1,400 fps. Feed reliability is good, and the cartridge is about as strong as loads fired in the average 4-inch-barreled .357 Magnum revolver. I have handloaded the 115-grain Gold Dot to a full 1,500 fps without problems, with excellent results. Feed reliability is better than the .45, due to the angle of the bullet. You cannot simply load the Super to 9 x 23mm pressure; the 9 x 23 has a much stronger case and has been purposely designed to safely generate the performance it exhibits. The 9 x 23mm definitely has an advantage over the .38 Super, but recoil remains at a level that allows excellent control. The problem with the 9 x 23 is that brass and ammunition are more difficult to find and more expensive than for some other calibers.

LOADS FOR THE 9 X 23MM

(Five-inch Colt)		
Winchester Action Powder, 8.8 grains	124-grain Hornady XTP	1,439 fps
Winchester WSL, 5.0 grains	115-grain Silvertip	1,181 fps
(Practice)		

.40 SMITH & WESSON

This popular stubby round is a better cartridge than the 9mm, although its accuracy is adequate, at best, in my experience. It is shorter than the .45 ACP and I simply don't trust a cartridge that is shorter than the original .900-inch-long .38 and .45 ACP to feed reliably into the 1911 format. Every 9mm 1911 I have fired has been reliable, however, so there is a possibility I am mistaken. This said, the .40 is an adequate defense cartridge and can be more accurate in the 1911 than when fired in the general run of service-type pistols of other makes.

The .40-caliber does have a good reputation in law enforcement. As an example, the Cor-Bon 135-grain JHP, at 1,320 fps, has earned a particularly good reputation for effect on felons. So has the heavier Winchester 155-grain Silvertip. A good point in favor of the .40 is that bullets can be "long-loaded" or seated to a longer overall length in the 1911 than in other pistols. This allows for more powder capacity with no greater pressure, but imparts a greater velocity with a given bullet. Personally, I would rather have a .40-caliber 1911 than any Glock or SIG, but I still prefer other calibers. If you are swearing off the Glock, and have a drum full of brass, the .40-caliber 1911 may be a good idea.

10MM & .41 MAGNUM

These two cartridges, intended as law enforcement cartridges, failed, but survive to this day by the skin of their teeth. Both the .41 Magnum and the 10mm. had credible endorsements from respected gun writers and law enforcement officers, but each learned a lesson in humility when the calibers did not reach their original promise. The 10mm is a favorite of mine,

largely because it is available in good auto-pistols. The original 10mm was the Bren Ten, a strengthened and enlarged CZ 75-type pistol. When the Bren Ten introduction failed, both Colt and Smith & Wesson introduced pistols to fire this cartridge, thus keeping it alive. The 10mm at one point was considered for the standard FBI cartridge. For many reasons hotly debated by those with little law enforcement experience, the 1986 "Miami Massacre" (actually in south Dade County), which involved a firefight and the murder of two FBI agents, led to the adoption of different arms and calibers by the nation's leading criminal investigation agency.

While the FBI special agents in question certainly displayed courage and audacity, the performance of their ammunition left much to be desired. These brave men were armed with small-caliber handguns, the .38 Special and the 9mm. Ultimately, the Bureau decided to adopt a big-bore cartridge. The FBI felt that the .45 ACP kicked too much and had too little penetration. There is room for argument, but at the time there were few truly effective handgun bullets available that offered a balance of expansion and penetration. The 10mm was built on a large frame, or a .45-caliber-size handgun. Penetration was the watchword of the day and early 10mm ammunition had it in spades. Some of the rounds were really too hot for police use, producing as much as 1,200 fps with a 200-grain bullet. Yet the foreign-produced hollow-points that enjoyed early distribution were underdeveloped and failed to expand when put to the test. The FBI finally chose a Federal Hydra Shock in 180-grain weight, loaded to only 980 fps. This seemed acceptable for defense, and full-power rounds could be carried in a spare magazine. The advent of the .40 Smith & Wesson, which offered basically the same performance as the FBI's reduced-power load, killed the 10mm in law enforcement. The .40 could be chambered in 9mm frame handguns; the 10mm requires a .45-sized handgun frame.

The 10mm has good power and excellent penetration with proper loads. In my testing only the .357 SIG comes close in penetration, but the 10mm eases the .357 SIG out. Using a good hollow-point, like the Hornady XTP, you have a cartridge with enough velocity to ensure good bullet performance. The 10mm can be gilt-edged accurate. Like the .357 Magnum, the full-power 10mm can be hard on a gun. Practice with milder loads and the gun will last much longer. The first Colt Delta Elite pistols had a service life as short as 5,000 rounds with full-power ammunition. By using heavy recoil springs and shock buffs, the situation can be improved, but all in all the full-power 10mm is at its best in occasional use. If you are comfortable with the .40-caliber Smith & Wesson's power level, the FBI load or Federal Hydra Shock at 980 fps is controllable and accurate. If you need the power to drop a deer or perhaps deliver the coup de grace to a downed boar, the 10mm XTP load from Hornady will serve. The most powerful commercially produced 10mm ammunition comes from Texas Ammunition. This includes a 135-grain JHP at 1,450 fps, 165-grain JHP at 1,350 fps, and a 200-grain flat-point (Horandy) bullet loaded to a full 1,250 fps.

.400 COR-BON

The .400 Cor-Bon differs from the 10mm in that the cartridge can be fired in standard .45 ACP pistols with only a barrel change. The .400 Cor-Bon is simply a .45 ACP case necked down to .40 caliber. The necked-down case allows greater case capacity and feed reliability as well. The .400 Cor-Bon is not the equal of the 10mm when the older cartridge is loaded to full power levels, especially with 180-grain bullets. The .400 Cor-Bon cannot efficiently use bullets over 165 grains. But with these bullets, the cartridge is a real hummer. I have used the .400 Cor-Bon a fair amount over the years, with generally good results. It is best to use factory ammunition in this caliber for defense, but Starline now offers good brass for reloaders. I have managed to work the 135-grain Nosler bullet up to a solid 1,425 fps in five-inch-barrel guns.

Accuracy is good to outstanding. I have far less experience with the 150-grain loads, but 1,300 fps is not out of the question. The heavier 165-grain Sierra bullets give 1,250 fps. This is good performance, and in every case the bullets show good expansion and even fragmentation. I think the cartridge has merit, but at present we have only one ammunition supplier and the caliber is basically aftermarket. Frankly, I don't see anything it will do that the 10mm can't do, and a lot that the 10mm can do with heavy bullets that the .400 Cor-Bon could never do. But the .400 Cor-Bon is a lot of gee-whiz that can be fired in the .45 by simply plugging in the barrel.

.45 SUPER

It had to come from Texas! The Super is an attempt by ammunition designers to improve the ballistic characteristics of the .45 ACP and is a rousing success. The first concern is gun-wear, but it seems that properly set up 1911s in .45 Super are running thousands of rounds without problems. Apparently, the 10mm did not come set up correctly from the factory, but the custom Supers are sprung correctly. I have fired quite a bit of ammunition from Texas Ammunition with excellent results. Basic ballistics include a 185-grain JHP at 1,250 fps and a 230-grain JHP at 1,075 fps. Some 230-grain loads have delivered more velocity in the 1,125 fps level. Recoil is certainly there but so is ballistic effect.

This 1911 inch .45 Super is from Ace Hindman's shop in Kerrville, Texas.

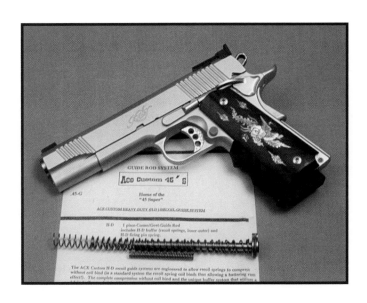

The Super case is identical to the standard .45 ACP in appearance, but is much stronger. You cannot load .45 Super loads in a standard .45 ACP case, at least not safely. I think this cartridge answers the need for additional penetration well. The .45 Super will equal the .357 Sig or 10mm in penetration but with a heavier, more effective bullet. The Hornady XTP was wisely chosen by Texas Ammunition as the bullet of choice in its .45 Super loads. This bullet expands dramatically at .45 Super velocities without giving up penetration. The recoil of the Super is stout, but not quite wrist snapping. Accuracy can be extremely good, partly due to the well-designed pistols that fire this cartridge.

78

MODEL
1911
MODEL
1911
MODEL
1911
MODEL
1911
MODEL
1911
MODEL
1911
MODEL
1911
MODEL
1911
MODEL
1911
MODEL
1911
MODEL
1911
MODEL
1911
MODEL
1911
MODEL
1911
MODEL
1911
MODEL
1911
MODEL
1911
MODEL
1911
MODEL
1911
MODEL
1911
MODEL
1911
MODEL
1911
MODEL
1911
MODEL
1911
MODEL
1911
MODEL
1911

RANGE DRILLS

Calm, deliberate practice and a good instructor pay big dividends.

Anyone who wonders why I hold the 1911 in such great esteem, need only take a few runs on the combat course. There is a reason for the 1911's popularity in all types of pistol competition. It is simply a wonder compared to most pistols, and second to none. When we decide to carry a handgun, we must be aware of the need for practice. Practice should include repetition of basic combat drills, and the shooter must master the basics of stance, grip, trigger press, sight picture, sight alignment, and follow-through.

A book can't teach you to shoot, they say — or can it? Frankly, most of what I have learned that was worthwhile about combat shooting I have learned from what I have read. The police training I received was primitive at best. The clear, incisive arguments of authors like Colonel Cooper and the various principles laid down by his disciples gave me a good groundwork for handgun shooting. Works by the old masters, Chic Gaylord, Paul Weston, Bill Jordan, and Ed McGivern were also helpful. Given proper groundwork, you can become a proficient handgun shot on your own. Some training is best, but you can do it. The single most helpful advice I can give is to attend IDPA (International Defensive Pistol Association) matches. Nowhere else will you find a better bunch of shooters who are willing to share helpful advice and give a hand on instruction. Safety rules are strictly enforced and gun handling demands are high. This practice can also be very enjoyable.

A shooter displays the proper grip on this Springfield 1911.

The basics include a good grip on the handgun. Here, we don't want to take a grip that will turn the grips to mush, but we do want to grip the weapon tightly. The 1911 grip safety must be properly depressed for the weapon to fire. And remember, any semiauto demands a strong platform to recoil against in order for the weapon to perform the recoil cycle properly.

When gripping the handgun, I often use the competitor's grip. This is 40 percent of the grip pressure in the hand holding the gun and 60 percent in the supporting hand. The supporting hand is cupped over the strong hand, with the thumbs either interlocked or pointing forward. High thumbs aid in recoil control, low thumbs in trigger control. You will find your balance. To learn the proper grip, grasp the gun until the hands tremble, then ease off pressure until you find a comfortable, firm grip. When the handgun is properly gripped, you will be able to use the sights properly and press the trigger straight to the rear, as designed.

Trigger compression is perhaps the single most difficult skill to develop. The trigger must be smoothly and quickly pressed, straight to the rear, without disturbing the sight picture. The trigger should break by surprise — we cannot say, "now is the moment it breaks," we press the trigger until the gun fires. Then we release the trigger and prepare for the next shot. In rapid fire, it is important that the press and release be in the same rhythm for maximum speed and accuracy.

Sight alignment is the proper alignment of the front and rear sights. The front post should be exactly centered in the rear sight, with equal light on each side and the top of the three parts of the picture equal. Sight picture is the superimposition of the sight on the target. Never do area aiming

REQUIREMENTS FOR ACHIEVING PROFICIENCY

Let's look at some of the requirements for achieving proficiency with the 1911. Among the skills we need to have in our tactical arsenal are:

- A winning mind-set most of all!
- Proper handling to prevent accidental discharges.
- Proper presentation of the weapon.
- Rapid reloading.
- The ability to fire at moving targets.
- The ability to fire from different positions.
- Proper use of cover.

This shooter (below left) has his thumbs locked one over the other, in order to aid in controlling the pistol's recoil.

The Weaver stance (above) is stable when properly executed.

or aiming at a whole target. That is a recipe for a miss. Aim at a certain distinct part of the target. The sights should be just below the target. With good sight alignment and a proper sight picture, and the trigger pressed smoothly we will have a hit.

Follow-through is maintaining control of the weapon as it fires. This is important because the gun recoils while the bullet is still in the barrel. That is the reason why sights are higher than the bore line. Follow-through is also important because we will be ready for a follow-up shot. Follow-through is a difficult skill for some shooters to master since they seem to jump when the gun fires, but it is very important.

The exact stance used is widely debated, but as long as the stance used is a solid two-hand stance, and the body is positioned for support, the stance the student finds most comfortable is acceptable. The Weaver stance, popularized by Jeff Cooper, remains a mainstay for the author. I took it to heart at an early age and assume the Weaver automatically, without thought. Since I was primarily responsible for my sons' training until I turned them over to various outstanding officers in service of Uncle Sam, this preference for the Weaver is reflected in these young men.

Care must be exercised when unloading and loading the weapon.

To take up the Weaver, we place our weak foot forward as if giving a forward punch. The gun hand stretches to full extension then the weak hand draws the gun back and the elbow of the weak hand dips. The arms act as shock absorbers. The Weaver is very solid and a good firing position. In the isosceles triangle, the arms are simply thrust forward, each about equally. This is an acceptable stance that many shooters find fast, comfortable, and accurate. Again, whatever works is best for the individual.

The single most significant shortcoming of new students is a lack of familiarity with the handgun. The most vital factor in short-range gunfights is gun handling. The accuracy problem is seldom severe, but speed into action and positive manipulation are imperative.

Safety always comes first. To avoid accidental discharges, safety rules must be enforced. There are many, but the basics are to keep the muzzle pointed downrange at all times, assume each gun is always loaded, and keep the trigger finger off the trigger until ready to fire: not when you think you will fire but when you actually fire. Any shooter should commit these rules to heart from the beginning. If you are caught up in a critical incident, these handling skills can save your life. Keep the finger off the trigger until you fire! Keeping the finger just outside the trigger guard, above the trigger guard, or slightly bent and away from the trigger guard will avoid an accidental discharge but will not compromise speed.

At this point we will look at several drills that may prove useful on the streets. On the range, we have plenty of time to think about what we are doing, and the stress level is not very high. But the concepts that are learned on the range will be firmly set in our minds and we will not have to think about what to do in the event that we are confronted by armed assailants. An important skill is the draw. I know beyond a shadow of a doubt that a rapid presentation of the weapon saved my life on two occasions. On the street, the adversary has marked his target and will attack with the weapon in hand. We must react… and react quickly.

Step 1: The hand shoots to the handgun to draw the weapon.Note that the trigger finger is well outside the holster.

Step 2: A draw begins.

Step 3: The weapon is fired from belt level.

At first, all practice drills should be carried out with a properly double-checked, unloaded weapon, before gradually progressing to range drills with live ammunition. The proper draw begins with the gun holstered. If the holster has a safety snap, then it must be fastened, since this is how the gun is normally carried in service. We are striving for smoothness first of all; speed comes with practice. The 1911 is long and flat and draws quickly. The techniques I use should work for most shooters. I shoot the elbow to the rear and the hand falls on the weapon, the grip is affirmed and the gun is brought from the holster. To move your hand to the gun, stop, and then draw is much slower. With the elbow-to-the-rear draw, the gun comes out of the holster, the hands meet at navel level in a two-hand hold, and the gun is pushed toward the target. A good standard is to be able to draw, fire, and strike a man-sized target with a solid center hit at ten yards in one and one-half seconds. This is not fast or slow but adequate. It takes time to get there.

There are two useful self-defense tactics that are used at very close range. The Speed Rock is a technique for stopping an adversary at point-blank range. The gun is drawn and fired just as it clears belt level. This is used when an adversary is literally on top of you in a situation such as a stabbing attack. It demands practice, especially in keeping the support hand clear of the muzzle, but it can be a lifesaver.

Every once in a while someone comes along with a new idea concerning point shooting or instinct shooting. No manner how many times we put this fallacy to rest, someone comes along arguing as if they were the first one to think of it. Let me simply ask you this. When an innocent bystander is wounded by "point shooting"— and Gaylord's *Handgunner's Guide* records numerous incidents —would you like to be the trainer who tells the jury: "I trained the shooter not to use his sights?" The Speed Rock is for contact shooting; the sights are for any range past bad breath distance.

There is another technique that is not point shooting but is very fast for close-range work. This is the Applegate Point. The gun is drawn and quickly pointed/aimed toward the adversary. The shooter looks toward the opponent. The moment the gun breaks the plane between the shooter and the target, the front sight is placed over the target and the gun is discharged. This is a brilliantly fast tactic that works well on the range. At seven to twelve feet it can save your life. Don't count on anything but the sights, however, at conversational distance and beyond.

The author practices night- fire drills.

Night shooting is a problem most service shooters will face. Many incidents occur in dim light or in darkened buildings, and they occur at very short range as well. For that reason, body position will usually carry the day. The stance and tactics used in daylight will work against an assailant a few feet away. Advanced training is needed to address a target at longer distances. If you carry a light, such as my personal choice, the Streamlight Scorpion, you will be prepared to illuminate and identify your target. The best tactic I have found is the Harries. In this shooting stance, the backs of the hands touch, with the support or weak hand on the outside of the strong-side hand. The light is held bulb end forward or pointed out of the back of the hand, and the thumb strikes the on-switch when illumination is needed. This is a strong firing stance, more than adequate for use at short range in dim light. It requires practice, especially since the hands can cross the muzzle of the 1911 if the student does not take due care. This is a good time to point out the advantages of a weapon that features both a manual safety and a grip safety.

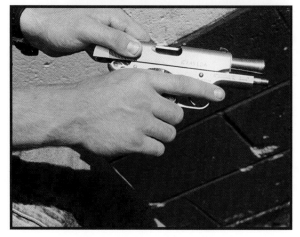

Racking the slide during TAP-RACK-BANG practice.

MALFUNCTION DRILLS

The 1911s do not malfunction often, but all mechanical devices are subject to failure at some point. When a 1911 does choke up, a simple drill will usually cure the problem. This is the well-known TAP-RACK-BANG. When you have a malfunction, you first TAP the magazine to be certain that it is properly seated, then RACK the slide back to clear any misfeed, normally tilting the weapon so that a jammed round can fall clear, and then comes the obvious — BANG!

Two of the most important tactical considerations consist of making yourself as small a target as possible and getting under cover. Those who have cover live. Cover is anything that will stop a bullet. This can mean the engine block of a vehicle, a large tree, or a fire hydrant. Concealment is a bush or a sheet on a clothesline. Cover is much better than concealment! When moving to cover, understand that the draw and movement conflict. Draw your gun and sprint or sprint to cover, then draw your gun, but don't draw on the run; you will be slow and awkward. Firing from cover is an important skill. With a minimum of bracing, firing from cover can be very accurate, especially when your nerves are rattled. Take care when bracing the weapon to be certain it does not actually touch the cover, but that your arms do.

Firing a Wilson Combat Close Quarters Battle around a corner.

If you are caught in the open, taking a low position is a worthwhile move. A move to kneeling or prone firing position strengthens your shooting stance and makes you a smaller target. Kneeling and prone moves should be practiced often to maintain proficiency. Remember, if the adversary has a height advantage, prone position can actually present a longer target.

SPEED RELOADING

Reloading is seldom necessary during a gun battle, but it can occasionally be necessary. The 1911 is among the fastest, if not the fastest, handguns of all time to recharge. There are two types of reloads commonly taught. Both require identical retrieval of the spare magazine. In the first case, the gun is run dry and the slide locks open. The weak hand drops quickly to the spare magazine, drawing the magazine with the forefinger held alongside the magazine. The magazine is brought to the weapon. Meanwhile,

TOP:
*A speedload with
a Springfield .45.*

BOTTOM:
*The author drops to
a prone firing position.*

with the firing hand, strike the magazine release and the magazine falls free. The spare is now inserted and the firing-hand thumb depresses the slide release, dropping the slide and loading the gun. I prefer the alternative of grasping the rear of the slide and releasing it to load the gun. This takes a few more seconds, but is more positive under stress.

The second speed load is the tactical load. The magazine has not been emptied but the weapon has been fired. The weak hand draws a magazine as the strong hand hits the magazine release. As the weak hand comes up to the pistol, the magazine in the weapon, which may have rounds in it, is taken in hand as the new magazine is inserted. The partially loaded magazine is saved. It is wise to have both reloading techniques firmly in your tactical arsenal.

The 1911 handles quickly and efficiently. Once you have gotten the feel of this gun, you can begin to plan a personal firing regimen. If your personal scenario calls for dealing with felons at longer ranges, you will need to practice for this possibility. Don't attempt to rely upon skills you cannot demonstrate. You will not rise to the occasion in a fight, but perform according to the best skills that you have demonstrated at the range. In a firing situation, I recommend always firing two shots, known as the double tap. This doubles the wound potential. The 1911 is capable of placing two hits on a target just about as quickly as one. But there are three types of doubles, all of which are useful in a crisis.

THE HAMMER

Two shots fired as quickly as possible without regard to sight alignment after the first shot — at very close range.

THE DOUBLE TAP

After the first round is fired, another shot is fired as the gun comes out of recoil and a coarse sight picture is taken. This is useful at three to ten yards.

THE CONTROLLED PAIR

Much like the double tap, but more time is taken with the second sight-picture, since greater care is demanded to strike a target at longer range. For 10 yards or more.

ALTERNATE ACTION TYPES OF THE 1911

85

MODEL 1911 MODEL

Three types of 1911 actions — single action, top; LDA, middle; and SFS, bottom.

For some time there has been an objection to the preferred mode of carry for the 1911, that is, the cocked-and-locked carry. The hammer is reared back and this gives some folks the jitters. Even more important, various police chiefs and administrators have condemned the carry. I would wager that some agencies that have gone to double-action-only pistols that have no manual safety wish they had adopted the "dangerous" 1911. The fact is that quite a few very experienced shooters prefer a double-action pistol. The double-action trigger both cocks and fires the weapon. The long first pull makes a manual safety unnecessary in the eyes of some, although I disagree. The late George C. Nonte stated that "simple readiness demands the pistol be brought into action without disengaging any safeties or levers." Nonte was more than a writer, he was a man with a military background, and a brilliant gunsmith as well. In the past, the double-action man had to have a Smith & Wesson or SIG. But now we have successful variants on the 1911 frame that allow both double-action and single-action/safe-action themes. There have been attempts at alternate action types in the past. Levers that cocked the hammer when pressed were tried. The Colt Double Eagle double-action pistol failed in practice and in the marketplace. Strangely, my experience with the Double Eagle, as far as accuracy and reliability go, has been good. But perhaps once the

The slide action cocks or preps the trigger of the LDA gun.

damage was done, the pistol could not overcome a bad reputation. The Double Eagle pistol featured a long draw-bar that used the trigger to cock and release the hammer. Here we have a considerable problem. A true double-action pistol places the trigger finger above the trigger guard, allowing the finger to sweep down and press the trigger to the rear. A single-action trigger need only be pressed straight back.

A double-action trigger fires the gun for the first shot, the slide then cocks the hammer, and the subsequent shots are fired single action. A double-action-only trigger fires each shot with a long pull of the trigger. The Para Ordnance LDA, or light-double-action trigger, is a true double-

The LDA trigger in its forwardmost position.

action only. When the gun is fired, the hammer rides down with the slide. The hammer cannot be cocked and the action of the slide sets the trigger. A long but relatively light pull of the trigger cocks the hammer and fires the weapon. The LDA trigger pull is difficult to describe but it is far nicer than a double-action revolver to most of us. It is more like a long-single-action trigger. The LDA demands practice and determination but I find that many shooters do speed work very well with this trigger. Rather than concentration, the LDA demands coordination. The LDA has been used in competition with excellent results. Overall, I find the action is usable for all-around shooting and excels in combat shooting. Having fired several examples with hard recoiling +P loads, I can attest to the ruggedness of the LDA action.

When the German National Police began their search for a new police pistol, they demanded an action without a safety. The double-action SIG was one winner, the double-action H and K P 9, which did not have to be carried on safe, were contenders, and the remarkable Heckler and Koch P7M8 another winner. The P7M8 is cocked by squeezing a lever in front of the grip, which cocks the action. In Europe, much research has gone into this type of action. A Safety Shooting System was developed for the Browning High Power, and eventually the system was applied to the 1911. The SFS system allows for carrying a 1911 ready to go by simply releasing the safety, but retains cocked-and-locked carry with the hammer down. Best of all, the SFS can be retrofitted to any existing 1911. I have had extensive experience with the SFS. Like most systems it has certain trade-offs, but overall the tactical advantages outweigh the shortfalls.

If the agency will not approve a 1911 that demands cocked-and-locked carry, there is little point in pressing the issue. In many agencies, hammer-down or empty-chamber carry of the .45 was allowed. The SFS is another matter. The SFS features an internal hammer ring. This ring is cocked in the normal fashion when the pistol's slide is racked and the external hammer also is cocked. However, the hammer can be pressed forward against spring pressure. As the hammer is pressed forward, the safety is pressed into safe position. A special block moves between the hammer and slide. To fire the gun, press the safety lever down in 1911 style. The hammer is released and springs to the rear. This amazes folks at the range but the novelty soon wears off.

The pistol is as quick into action as any 1911. While the SFS can be applied to any 1911, my personal handgun, the High Standard G Man, features the SFS as an option. An advantage is that the SFS gun can be kept at home, ready with the safety on and hammer down, but the hammer need not be cocked. (Do not lower the hammer manually, as you would on a 1911, by

LEFT:
This shows the long draw-bar that allows the Light Double Action trigger to function.

RIGHT:
Unlike many double-action-only designs, the LDA allows on-safe carry.

holding the hammer and pressing the trigger. This would then require that the hammer be cocked before the gun is fired, and short-circuits the safety. The gun can be carried chamber empty if desired).

A slight drawback to the SFS is that, in tactical movement, the safety cannot be pressed on. The hammer must be pressed forward to make the gun safe. This is a trade-off, but, in the end, it is a viable, effective system. For those desiring some other action type but feeling that the other qualities of the 1911 are worthwhile, the LDA guns are the choice in new factory production. In older guns, we can fit the SFS.

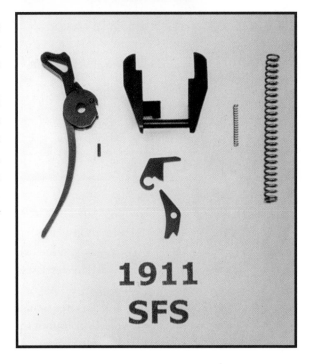

Parts of the SFS system.

88

MODEL
1911
MODEL
1911
MODEL
1911
MODEL
1911
MODEL
1911
MODEL
1911
MODEL
1911
MODEL
1911
MODEL
1911
MODEL
1911
MODEL
1911
MODEL
1911
MODEL
1911
MODEL
1911
MODEL
1911
MODEL
1911
MODEL
1911
MODEL
1911
MODEL
1911
MODEL
1911
MODEL
1911
MODEL
1911
MODEL
1911
MODEL

LEATHER FOR THE 1911

I began carrying a handgun on a daily basis nearly 35 years ago and much has changed since then. There were a few good holsters in those days, but I was not aware of them. Nelson, Kramer, and Blocker were yet to come. Concealment holsters were terrible and police-style belt holsters did not offer concealment. Ultimately, we saw a great deal of progress, seemingly overnight. Roy Baker's form-hugging pancake and Bruce Nelson's Summer Special were wonderful holsters, and are still well suited to the modern professional. Lou Alessi's DOJ and various concealment holsters raised the bar in quality. When life and death hangs in the balance, haphazard gear is not acceptable. Over the years I have used holsters of all types and formed a good idea of what works.

Because we are only concerned with the 1911, selection is a simple process. The long, flat 1911 is relatively easy to conceal. Many holsters work well with the 1911. Accept nothing but high-quality holsters. Double stitching, top-rated thread, a perfect fit, and good finish should be apparent. The holster mouth should be reinforced so that it will not collapse when the gun is drawn, and the belt loops or tunnels should be properly placed and sewn.

If you wish to show off, this Boa holster from Kramer is a holster of distinction.

Holster material is an important consideration. Among the best choices is high-grade leather. Leather is durable, can give an excellent fit, and survives hard use well. Horsehide was once viewed as an expensive, premium component, available only from the top makers. Today, High Noon Holsters offers quality horsehide at a minimal cost over other leather. Horsehide is tougher per ounce than cowhide and provides much better resistance to water. Horsehide also keeps its shape better with hard use. Overall, horsehide is a superior product, well worth the modest extra cost.

Space-age Kydex holsters are impervious to solvents, moisture, and oils. Some are cheaply made; others offer good to excellent fit. Some of the very best examples come from Hillsman Holsters, with good examples also coming from Blade Tech.

When considering holsters, it is best to discuss specific examples and evaluate how they perform. Quite a few designs are especially well suited to the 1911. There are four main types of holsters we will concern ourselves with. These are the strong-side holster, the cross-draw, the inside-the-pants holster, and the shoulder holster. There should always be a good reason for not choosing the strong side holster, as it is the most efficient and offers the greatest comfort and the quickest draw. But the others can serve well. Pocket holsters and ankle holsters are not suitable for even the smallest 1911.

There are two types of good belt holsters. These are the scabbard and the pancake. The scabbard is a more heavily built holster. The scabbard, on the other hand, gives us good speed, excellent retention, and offsets the gun from the body for comfort. If the angle is correct and the holster is worn properly, this holster can be concealed under a jacket. The pancake is usually made from a single piece of leather and rides close to the body, hugging our form for good concealment. The pancake is a good choice. The grip of the pistol is closer to the body, making the draw a bit more challenging, but a good sharp draw is possible with practice. The pancake spreads the weight of the gun out on the belt. There are a number of pancake holsters offering good function.

Don Hume produces a holster, the 721, that I have called the gunfighter's holster, or the holster of the century. This holster features thorough design excellence, good fit and finish, excellent retention, and real speed. The 721 uses tunnel belt loops for security. While available in an open-top version, many police agencies demand a thumb break for security and this is the type I have used most often. The holster features a speed slot cut in the front that allows a good hand to rock the gun forward and clear leather very quickly. The holster is simply excellent, a good holster and a good buy.

The belt-slide holster is a variation on the strong-side theme. This is simply a cut-down holster of minimal dimensions. I am not really pleased with these holsters, preferring more security, but Gallagher offers an example that gives a tight friction fit and good security. Another variation on the strong-side is the paddle holster. I am not really fond of these, either. The paddle is designed for easy on-and-off changing, designed for

Taurisano holster worn with an Auto Ordnance .45.

This paddle holster from Gould and Goodrich ranks high in the author's estimation.

federal agents and others who have to frequently enter jails, courtrooms, or other restricted areas. For the civilian who enters prohibited areas and has to remove a gun often, it has some appeal. I prefer a paddle that attaches to the belt. The Kramer Michigan State Police model is one, and Wild Bill makes another. A workman-like traditional paddle comes from

ABOVE:
This is an original Gordon Davis cross-draw that once belonged to an outlaw biker.

RIGHT:
An especially clean design from Gould and Goodrich.

Gould & Goodrich, a well-respected supplier of police leather.

This paddle is a good design, and in it the long, heavy 1911 does seem to lock into the hip well. Among the most recent paddle designs I have tested is the Speedy Spanky from High Noon Holsters. This holster is not only well made and more secure than most, but it offers a very fast draw. It is even available in horsehide!

One of the great 1911 holsters of all time was designed from the outset specifically for the 1911 pistol. When the Federal Bureau of Investigation's Hostage Rescue Unit adopted the 1911-type handgun, it had to have a good solid holster design well suited to carrying the pistol concealed. The DeSantis HRT was the result. This holster features solid, reinforced tunnel loops for mating solidly to the belt. There is a retention screw for adjustment of tension and a reinforced thumb-break that is among the best ever designed. This thumb-break is specific to the 1911 and a very good design. While the wearer is protected from the cocked hammer of the 1911, the holster offers real speed. You could do much worse than choosing this holster for your 1911.

With any holster design it is important that the holster be worn properly. The belt should be threaded through the loops so that the holster does not sag. Run the belt in a loop, through a belt loop in the pants, then through the final loop. This will make for much more comfortable wear and a steady draw. In no case is this more important than with the second holster we will consider, the cross-draw.

I have had extensive experience with a number of cross-draw holsters, including examples from Gordon Davis, Kramer, and Blocker. When it comes to cross-draw holsters, a bad one is very bad and a good one difficult to find. The cross-draw itself is often criticized but offers real advantages in certain situations. When seated behind a desk or in a vehicle, reaching across the body for a cross-draw is faster than reaching for a strong-side-mounted handgun. The cross-draw is slower than the strong side from a standing draw. Not only do we reach across the body, when the draw is completed we are sweeping across the target instead of into the target, with more chance for a miss. Just the same, many experienced shooters swear by the cross-draw.

Before we move to other types, I will briefly touch on police-duty holsters. I have been out of the business for a few years but there are good, solid holsters available from the same makers of the holsters that gave me good service. A strong, simple, but durable version from Gould & Goodrich has really proven a good choice in my latest test program. This holster features good retention, a fast but secure thumb-break, and an excellent finish. I have done several fast draws with this holster and worn it for several days as a test. It is a good choice for duty and certainly in anyone's top three service holsters.

Don Hume has listened to the needs of modern officers working the mean streets and introduced a holster known as the Street Guard. Intended for concealed carry, this holster offers good retention and speed. Practice, as always, is indicated. If I were working a burglary unit or other high-risk squad, this would be my first choice. The Street Guard requires a special motion to free the weapon, but once freed from this retaining block the holster allows for excellent speed. This is among my top three choices for concealed carry.

TOP:
The Speedy Spanky Paddle from High Noon — a good choice.

BOTTOM:
The Street Guard from Don Hume.

The number one choice of professionals worldwide is the inside-the-waistband holster. This holster rides between the trousers and the user's body. This causes the holster's one complaint – it can be uncomfortable. This is weighed against excellent concealment. When this holster is worn, a full-size handgun can be concealed under even light garments. Since the holster is buried in the pants, and does not extend past the belt line, even a light windbreaker will conceal a government-model .45. This makes for great advantages for civilians and peace officers alike. I used this carry almost exclusively for over 20 years, and it works very well.

Like many of the best designs, the first truly effective IWB holster was designed by a working cop. Bruce Nelson designed the immortal Summer Special. The Summer Special features a built-in sight track, a reinforced holster mouth to prevent the holster from collapsing after the gun is drawn, and double belt loops. This is an excellent choice, especially for short .45s. There are several good IWBs, especially the Taurisano and Kramer models, and anyone should be able to find a version that suits their needs.

Michael Taurisano is a retired cop of some reputation who sells handcrafted holsters of unmistakable quality. He makes an IWB with offset double loops and a strong double spine. This holster really takes the load off when carrying a 1911 on a 24-hour basis. I cannot recommend this holster highly enough.

Shoulder holsters have many adherents, but are very much a personal choice. I have used the DeSantis brand in many versions, always with good service. Possibly one of the better examples is the 030, a holster of dull black construction that is low key and very, very well made. The New York Undercover is another good choice, preferably for lighter weapons. I have used a special version of the shoulder holster from High Noon for some time. It offers good adjustment, a dual magazine carrier, and is well made of thick cowhide.

This Graham Gun leather Saigon belt clip holds the author's Commander .45.

Purchasing a good holster is perhaps only half the battle. A good shoulder holster demands proper adjustment. Some men find the shoulder holster stifling and simply cannot adapt to it. I like the shoulder holster because it moves the gun off the belt, takes pressure off the back, and offers efficient allocation of defense gear. That is what holster selection is all about — allocation of space. Don't crowd the belt with cell phones, pagers, or other gear. You may regret it at a later date.

The proper method of wearing an IWB Taurisano holster.

TESTING THE 1911

93

MODEL
1911
MODEL
1911
MODEL
1911
MODEL
1911
MODEL
1911
MODEL
1911
MODEL
1911
MODEL
1911
MODEL
1911
MODEL
1911
MODEL
1911
MODEL
1911
MODEL
1911
MODEL
1911
MODEL
1911
MODEL
1911
MODEL
1911
MODEL
1911
MODEL
1911
MODEL
1911

This book would not have been complete without test-firing the 1911; indeed a large part of the book is composed of the results of these tests. While history and mechanical examination are interesting, we are first and foremost concerned with the pistol's performance on the range in reality-based drills. I have had a marvelous opportunity while working with various periodicals to review, examine, and test-fire a hundred or so 1911 pistols over the past ten years. I kept careful notes during my work, and many of the pistols had practically every shot carefully recorded. The work stretches over more than a decade. You may note that my enterprising and overworked sons helped me. They have been invaluable in testing and evaluating handguns and also in handloading.

I have always been interested in tests and evaluation and these tests have by no means been limited to the 1911. Over the years, I have examined many good and reliable weapons, but the more I test competing designs, the more I am certain that the 1911 is the superior pistol. By the same token, the 1911 is not for everyone. The 1911 is not for those who are disinterested in training or unwilling to learn. The pistol will not suffer fools lightly — but then no weapon will for long.

This box contains several thousand rounds of new Remington UMC.

When testing a handgun, the foremost criterion is reliability. We have seen many pretty guns that were not reliable and I have seen some ugly guns that showed gilt-edged accuracy. Then, we have the average 1911, which is a credible weapon with a good balance of reliability and accuracy. As I formed my opinions, I began to put much of what I learned to paper.

Some have asked the path to becoming a firearms writer. Being well read is important, if only to acquaint yourself with the confusing doctrines that exist and the pitfalls of "non-information" pathways. But hands-on experience is necessary. Before I penned my first article, I had 20 years of handgun experimentation and use under my belt. Much of what I had seen in print I questioned. Some of the conclusions were illogical and showed little connection with reality. At the same time, there was much good information forthcoming from Skeeter Skelton, Jeff Cooper, Elmer Keith, Bill Jordan, George C. Nonte, Tom Ferguson, and Chuck Taylor. Later, Dave Spaulding, Denny Hansen, and Chris Pollack were among my favorite authorities. These writers are intelligent men of varied interests who share extensive backgrounds in either military or police service. They all have one thing in common — what they write is verifiable. They have no secret sources. They simply tell of their experiences. The experiences they have had, and the range drills they have performed, can be repeated by the reader. I did so in many cases and found them correct, although I usually formed my own opinions.

Keith and Jordan, as an example, had little use for semiauto pistols. But their recommendation of powerful handguns and straight shooting were well taken. Once I became a peace officer, there was much fertile ground for investigation. When a peace officer tells you he has seen many shootings, what he means is that he has arrived just after they were over, often with the victim or shooter still kicking or screaming. And few of these shootings are clear-cut, with the victim usually meeting the perpetrator halfway. So many of the opinions I have on handgun performance are based on reality.

The author's assistant, Matthew Campbell, wears eye and ear protection for the tests.

As for the test guns, only by building a solid reputation over many years can you ask for test gear with a reasonable expectation of the request being granted. Most of the guns tested, perhaps 85 percent, were either personal guns or the guns of my friends and associates.

To test handguns, we had to have a model on which to base procedure. All the pistols had to be tested consistently. Pistols tend to be tested in the same habitual way by most journal testers, and most of the time they are wrong. There are alternate test programs, and I attempted to use a smattering from each. The obligatory 25-yard testing — firing the handgun from a solid bench-rest for grouping ability — may be the least important of these tests. Firing a pistol from a machine rest is as far removed from reality and combat shooting as possible. A machine rest does not respect the nuances of a bad trigger, sharp edges, or a tang that bites the hand. Yet these flaws would never be discovered if testing were confined to machine rest firing. Such methods are a good test of handgun ammunition, but then again, the major makers have test barrels for that purpose. I suppose a dedicated handloader — which I am — in pursuit of excellence should have a machine rest for test firing his handgun. None of the guns tested, even the smallest, most compact weapons, lacked the accuracy necessary for defense. But if we had compared machine rest groups of small and large guns, in many cases the small guns would have bested the five-inch-barrel government models.

In the reality of range shooting, the small frame guns are not even roughly as capable as the full-length models. The ability to control the weapon in rapid fire and make rapid, multiple hits on multiple targets is greatly decreased by going to a compact weapon. A machine rest or 25-yard bench-rest simply does not show these shortcomings. Don't misunderstand; the compact .45s are good, concealable weapons far superior to any short-barrel revolver or a small-caliber handgun. But they bear the same relationship to a full-length 1911 that a snub-nosed .38 does to a full-size revolver. The compact .45s are good, but no substitute for a Government Model handgun. When I work in a new service gun, I do sight it in off the bench with the load of choice, but I don't fire endless groups. I fire the gun at various targets of unknown distance in an attempt to build speed in combat shooting drills. Once the zero is confirmed, this is the correct course for a practical handgunner.

To adequately test combat potential, we adopted a number of drills in testing the 1911s. Two were modeled after the tests conducted in various magazine articles, and Bill Wilson pop-

The author's version of braced firing. Firing from an upright rest.

ularized another. Over 10 years ago, I was surprised to see that a writer named Denny Hansen did not test handguns at a bench rest from 75 feet. Hansen is the editor of *SWAT* Magazine. A double Kevlar survivor, Hansen is a former police officer of long experience. He fires his handguns in volleys of 10 rounds at 10 yards and measures the group. Most good handguns of the 1911 type will group into about three inches in this drill. This demonstrates control and practical accuracy better than a bulls-eye group. On the rest, poor sights and a heavy trigger can be dealt with by an experienced shooter — off hand they are much more of a problem.

The Bill Drill was made popular by Bill Wilson, an extraordinary gunsmith and competitor. In this drill, we draw and fire at a target placed at seven yards and fire six rounds as quickly as possible. This drill is fired against time. With a Competition Electronics timer, I was able to measure controllability and the shooter's skill. We fired the Hansen drill and the Bill Drill with each pistol, usually several times, in order to get an average. Finally, we fired several groups off the bench rest in order to qualify accuracy. We were careful, but our results in no way match those of a machine rest, and they should not. But they do show true accuracy potential.

GUN TESTS

Notes on the short .45s

I have arranged the test-fire results of the compact guns first. It seemed logical and, as it happens, most of them were tested toward the end of the test period. I would have liked to have included the Star PD, but in my experience 500 rounds is a big portion of a PD's lifetime and few owners would have consented. I long ago replaced my Stars with more rugged pistols. The PD was OK, but there are better guns. The new small .45s are much tougher than the PD. I mean this as no disrespect to one of the top guns of its time — the PD saved me from death or serious injury on two occasions. I carried the PD for 10 years. It fired in my defense and gave good service overall, but it wore too badly to trust after only 2,500 rounds of ammunition. In a 500-round test I would have had to replace the guide rod and buffer of the PD if indeed the gun would have lasted in that type of test. The PD may have lasted forever kept in a dresser drawer or under a counter, but I practiced hard with my 1911s. The gun did not fail; it simply exhibited eccentric wear and lost its accuracy. I had carried it so close to my body for so long that perspiration had permeated its internal workings and rusted them. One day I could not unload the gun — it was frozen shut due to a worn lug or link. I had to shoot the chambered round to unload the gun. I then retired it honorably.

The short 1911 pistols are leagues ahead of a compact 9mm handgun or a snub-nose .38, but the whole picture must be kept in perspective. My experience indicates that the short guns are not as reliable or long-lived as the five-inch-barrel Government Model. Also, the short sight radius of the compact guns makes accurate shooting more difficult, and the guns kick more. The gun is more "whippy" in the hand, requiring greater concentration to stay on target. This is proven by rapid-fire drills and measuring the "wobble factor." No one can honestly shoot a short .45 as quickly or as accurately as a full-length gun. The circle of dispersion is always larger and dictates the range at which it is safe to take a shot. If you can carry a Government Model or a Commander, do so, but sometimes our personal comfort level leads us toward a compact 1911. What we are looking for is a handgun capable of stopping a fight but is, at the same time, comfortable to carry for extended periods.

Colt began modifying various 1911s prior to World War II, finally unveiling the aluminum-frame, shortened Commander pistol in 1949. (One of the first was presented to ally and firearms enthusiast Winston Churchill — how times have changed!) The Commander is a good, sensible gun. But today we have much shorter and lighter guns. The Officers Model types are shortened in the butt as well as the slide, and the butt is what protrudes when the gun is carried concealed. We give up one round in ammunition capacity and some ammunition effectiveness when going to the compact pistols. I have no problem with these trade-offs since the guns are light to carry and retain sufficient power to get the job done. But reliability is a concern.

The compact pistols radically alter the pivot of Browning's tilting barrel, putting stress on the link. Because the slide is lighter, slide velocity is increased and so is battering. This is why many short .45s featured "coned" barrels and no barrel bushing. To control slide velocity, the slide recoils farther than in the case of a Government Model pistol. The wider front of the slide allows the slide to travel over the short barrel, which may have a locking lug deleted from the design for this purpose. The coned barrel allows a more severe tilt in action.

Spring-within-a-spring technology has answered the problem of slide velocity to some extent. The military was the first to develop a full-length guide rod, when the General Officer's pistol was designed, and many compact pistols feature this type of guide rod. Short barrel geometry determined much of the technology we see in use today. No-bushing lockup, coned barrels, full-length guide rods, shock buffs, and even one-piece magazine followers were developed in order to ensure reliability in the short 1911.

My experience with the short .45s is mixed. Two test pistols, the Colt 1991A1 Compact and the Kimber Ultra Carry, have proven reliable over time with any round tested. However, the same has not been true of certain examples of short .45s. My recommendation in the short .45s is to use 230-grain bullets. The lighter bullets seem to give less slide impetus and often fail to fully feed, especially on the last round. Magazines for the compact guns are frequently offered in seven-shot format. The spring must be weaker to accommodate the last round. I recommend six-round Metalform magazines in these guns. What good is the extra round if you have a malfunction?

Matthew Campbell firing on the combat course in IDPA competition.

More on Testing

We attempted to fire a representative example of four types of ammunition in each pistol, not necessarily in equal portions.

1. Handloads: designed for economy and to lessen wear on the pistol. By doing so we voided any warranty on the handguns. But if a pistol does not function with handloads, it is no good to me, as it cannot be fired economically. (Many competitors fire this amount of ammunition in a single year of practice sessions.) Our handloads were for the most part loaded lighter than factory ammunition in order to decrease wear on the pistols, but some were true +P loads, solid hunting loads that have performed well. The handloads used in testing are described by bullet and powder, but not always the exact powder charge.

2. Hardball: the standard .45 ACP load. We used numerous handload equivalents but relied for the most part on factory ammunition in this genre. Almost all were standard 230-grain ball loads. We also used some factory 200-grain SWC loads, which fit in roughly the same power category.

3. Service loads: various hollow-point loads intended for personal defense or police service use. If the handgun will not perform with modern expanding ammunition, its utility is severely limited.

4. +P loads: give the .45 an extra margin of power. Older guns were not always tested with +P loads, out of respect for older steel.

FIVE HUNDRED ROUNDS AND BEYOND

Handguns tested to 500 rounds and beyond fired this type of course:

300 ROUNDS

50 rounds	one hand	shoulder point	7 yards
50 rounds	two hands	any style	10 yards
50 rounds	two hands	rapid fire	10 yards
50 rounds	two hands	any style	15 yards
50 rounds	two hands	any style	25 yards
50 rounds	two hands	barricade	25 yards

Long ago I decided that 500 rounds is a minimum test of a handgun's reliability, and that this amount of ammunition is needed in order to get a good evaluation. This was the minimum that I tested in the majority of the handguns. In a number of cases, we fired 1,000 – 2,000 rounds in given weapons. Many of these pistols are long-term test guns, and have fired many more than the specified number of rounds. A few guns were fired less than 500 rounds out of respect for the owners. They were for sale and there was no point in pressing our luck. So the performance of these pistols cannot be judged as accurately as those guns that went the "Full Monte" and delivered 500 trouble-free rounds.

The majority of the rounds fired were in combat courses. This made shooting far more enjoyable. I seriously doubt a tranquilized gorilla could fire 500 rounds of .45 ACP off the bench-rest in a single weekend and not develop a trembling flinch. On the other hand, combat drills are much easier on the hands and nerves.

The handguns fired past 500 rounds were subjected to roll-over prone firing and even firing at 50 yards and beyond.

This test program gave us an excellent idea of the capabilities of any handgun. The majority of tests were undertaken during the past five years, which gave more consistency in the types of ammunition used. Still, among the older tests, you will notice that certain bullets and ammunition were no longer available. The test is just as viable with this ammunition as the original 1911 test was. We seriously considered firing one 1911 to 6,000 rounds to duplicate the original test, but with the FBI test program just over, with 25,000 rounds fired in several weapons without a problem, the 1911 was proven again. We thought it better to perform several smaller tests of a large number of 1911s. Frankly, we barely made it as far as ammunition was concerned. More than once, we rushed to the loading bench and cranked out rounds in anticipation of a weekend test and even found our way to Wal Mart to purchase one more box of USA ball a few times.

> # +P AMMUNITION
>
> We fired a total of 300 mixed rounds in +P ammunition. There were no malfunctions of any type, good accuracy, and not completely wrist snapping recoil. A couple of times we heard the mainspring coiling up like a chainsaw.
>
> **FIRED:**
>
> | | |
> |---|---|
> | 100 | Cor-Bon 165-grain +P |
> | 100 | Cor-Bon 185-grain +P |
> | 100 | Texas Ammunition 230-grain Tactical |

Someone said that many 1911s are not as reliable with +P ammunition as some other pistol and noted that Cor-Bon ammunition was too hot for reliable function. We lightly lubed a clean High Standard pistol with Birchwood Casey gun oil, loaded up our W. C. Wolff magazines, and did the following test. Texas Ammunition Tactical .45 is even hotter than Cor-Bon, loaded in .45 Super cases for strength — an excellent full-power load.

We were blessed with an embarrassment of riches, not only from our old friends at the Big Three, Speer, and Black Hills, but from new names such as Lancer and Weber. Cor-Bon supplied the majority of the +P-rated ammunition. I have to admit I enjoyed the handloading immensely. Along the way, I experimented with several loads. Being a writer, I worked up several articles on handloading for the .45 or the 1911 along the way. Some are real tack drivers. Without Sierra, West Coast Bullets, Montana Gold, Hornady, Oregon Trail, and others I would not have accomplished these monumental projects. All in all, this was an enjoyable experience, a learning experience par excellence, but, as we say in the South, a lot like work. Some of the guns were so similar I could forget which one I was shooting. But there were others that stood out. My favorites? Read on. What follows may step on some toes, but these are the facts. Each of these tests is repeatable and verifiable. Five hundred rounds of hardball is not that expensive, and you really should establish your 1911's reliability. Repeat these tests carefully, and do not fire simply to enjoy the noise of the big ugly. Think about what is happening. I think you and I will probably reach a consensus. If not, well, there are enough 1911s to go around to suit anyone's taste.

In our testing we did not "stack up" malfunctions wantonly. If we determined that a pistol malfunctioned due to a faulty magazine, we replaced the magazine. If a gun did not feed a certain type of hollow-point, we stopped testing and moved to other types. Our original intention was simply to compare 1911s, but the exercise turned out to give excellent insight into checking used and older 1911s for problems. Springs and magazines gave problems, and this was duly recorded. All in all, most of the pistols were reliable. Some were extraordinary in performance.

We fired accuracy tests from a hand-held rest on a sandbag. The majority of rounds were fired off hand, at seven to fifteen yards, on combat courses. As an example, a couple of the thumb-in-the-slide malfunctions would have been undetected if we had not fired the guns off hand. The rough tangs of several guns would have gone undiscovered. Also, trigger operation means a lot in firing any handgun, and off-hand fire tells the tale. I had plenty of help in firing the pistols, and we rated all guns in four important categories.

Test Categories:

Operation of controls — How crisp was the slide lock safety, did the grip safety work quickly and easily when depressed, did the slide lock stick?

Fit and Finish — The quality of the finish and the fit of all parts.

Trigger Compression — Not just the weight, but the absence of creep and backlash.

Sights — Military-type sights rated a universal "poor," but others were very good indeed, with most in between. High-visibility sights are needed for best use of the 1911.

Sharp Edges — The bane of the 1911 is sharp edges. This is not as important on a military weapon but very important when the pistol is carried for personal defense.

Ratings:

Excellent: in general, custom quality

Good: Above average

Fair: Better than military standard sights, perhaps average in trigger action.

Poor: Substandard

Signature groups were fired from a 25-yard bench-rest.

Hansen groups were five rounds at ten yards, rapid fire. The group of five rounds was measured from the center to center of the farthest apart bullet holes.

To understand the ratings you have to understand the Colt's manual of arms and operation. The 1911 has a slide lock safety and grip safety. The trigger compression is a single-action type, straight to the rear compression. When rating the controls, we considered the operation of the thumb safety, the slide lock, and the magazine release. All were required to be crisp and clean in operation, neither excessively stiff nor too light. Most pistols had controls that complemented each other, but some had nice triggers and poorly fitted controls or vice versa.

SAFETY CHECKS

If a pistol failed a safety check, no firing was considered. First, we triple-checked each weapon to be certain it was not loaded. Then we cocked the hammer and made certain it could not be pressed forward with finger pressure alone. Next, we racked the slide to the rear and locked it in place with the slide stop. We released the slide stop and let the slide run forward and slam on an empty chamber. This is abuse, pure and simple, but in no case did the hammer of any pistol fall off the full-cock notch and follow the slide down. To test the slide lock safety, I placed the gun on safe, depressed the grip safety, and pulled the trigger. The gun did not fire and neither did it fire when we placed the safety off. Next, I checked the grip safety by cocking the gun and pressing the trigger without depressing the grip safety. None of the pistols that we checked failed the safety test, but there were pistols found in numerous shops over the years that did fail, and were not purchased. The gun butcher can work his wonders and pass on the bill to others. I have never seen a factory gun with defective safety operation, but I have seen used 1911s that have been mangled.

Next, I disassembled each weapon and examined it for tool marks and workmanship. Some were rather rough but nonetheless worked; others were sterling examples of top-notch craftsmanship. Before testing, I lubricated each gun. I tried to be consistent in all factors, but time and the situation led to a variety of lubricants being used. Much can be said of the ammunition choice, but in the end we believe the eclectic choices made showed the practical reliability of the pistols far better than firing a single load 40,000 times would have. All in all, we think the test was fair and varied enough to give a credible and critical evaluation of the 1911 pistol as it exists at this time. Would I do it again? If the Lord gives me 10 more years, and the Big Three and others, and 40,000 rounds and if new 1911s continue to be introduced, of course I would!

102

MODEL
1911
MODEL
1911
MODEL
1911
MODEL
1911
MODEL
1911
MODEL
1911
MODEL
1911
MODEL
1911
MODEL
1911
MODEL
1911
MODEL
1911
MODEL
1911
MODEL
1911
MODEL
1911
MODEL
1911
MODEL
1911
MODEL
1911
MODEL
1911
MODEL
1911
MODEL
1911
MODEL
1911

TEST RESULTS

KIMBER ULTRA CARRY

Even if you don't like 1911s with short slides and barrels, the Ultra Carry can convert anyone. This is a well-made, credible weapon with much to recommend it. The problems associated with short-slide guns — sharp edges, unreliable function, and poor sights — are absent from this weapon. The beavertail safety makes for comfort and the sights allow

quick, accurate shooting. When firing the speed runs this pistol was quick on the target, but drifted off in rapid fire unless we concentrated intensely on the target. This is a function of the short sight radius and the gun's recoil. Recoil is there, but the gun is controllable. Don't compare the Ultra Carry to a full-sized .45. Compare it to the various snub-nosed .38s and compact 9mm pistols that are its direct competition. You will find that the Ultra Carry is a far better choice.

Our example showed excellent attention to detail. The finish of the flats of the slide was flawless. The controls were crisp and the pistol was smooth in operation.

Unlike many small pistols, the Ultra Carry could be an all-around defense gun. In the woods, on a hike, it is accurate enough to take out a reptile or feral dog or even put meat on the table, given a steady hand. Recoil was tiring to the wrists, as is to be expected from such a short, light .45. I found it remarkable that the pistol fired to the point of aim with almost all bullet weights, at least at moderate range.

Previously Fired:	New Gun	
Controls	E	
Fit and Finish	E	
Trigger	E	(4.5 lbs.)
Sights	E	
Sharp Edges	E	
Overall	E	

Malfunctions: *3 — These occurred when firing the +P loads twice and once with Lawman ball ammunition. The malfunction was shooter induced. When the gun was jolted in recoil, the weak side thumb bumped the magazine catch. This is common with light pistols and must be addressed by using a good solid firing grip.*

Signature Groups:
Montana Gold JHP handload	3.4 inches
230-grain Winchester JHP handload	4.0 inches
Hansen Drill: Speer Lawman	4.0 inches

Rounds Fired:

Montana Gold 230-grain JHP/231/840 fps	100
Montana Gold 230-grain FMJ/231/802 fps	100
Winchester 230-grain JHP/231/870 fps	100
Speer Lawman 230-grain FMJ	100
Fiocchi 200-grain JHP	50
Triton 165-grain JHP +P	50

We gave the Kimber a light cleaning at 250 rounds and liberally squirted Birchwood Casey gun oil on the inner workings. At 480 rounds, accumulated powder ash had made the gun sluggish in action but it worked, and accuracy remained good.

KIMBER CDP

The Custom Defense Package differed in few particulars from the Ultra Carry, and overall the performance was similar. The CDP featured a wilder beavertail and Kimpro finish on the frame. This was a borrowed gun and I had to run to get the test gun and get the shooting done, but the pistol impressed all of us with its performance. The single malfunction was probably due to a lack of lubrication: a push on the slide and the gun fired and kept running. When the gun was cleaned, it was really cruddy due to dirty handloads. I was glad to have a large bucket of Hoppes! Overall, I was impressed with this variation on the theme. Kimbers have given good results in all models, but I am still surprised to see small handguns perform so well. This was one of the few guns tested by itself, with no others for comparison during the range section. Overall, we found it well worth its price and a very good performer. The trigger was perhaps the best we ran across during the entire test program.

Previously Fired:	About 200 Rounds	
Controls	E	
Fit and Finish	E	
Trigger	E	(2.9 lbs.)
Sights	G	
Sharp Edges	E	
Overall	E	
Malfunctions	1 failure to fully lock the slide	

Signature Groups:

Sierra 230 JHP	4.0 inches
Fiocchi Ball	4.5 inches
Hansen Group: Fiocchi Ball	4.5 inches

Rounds Fired:

Sierra 230-grain JHP 230gr. JHP/231/840 fps	200
Fiocchi 230-grain ball	100
Houston Cartridge 230-grain Ball	100
Federal 230-grain Classic JHP	50
Cor Bon 200-grain JHP +P	50

COLT 1991 COMPACT

This is an example of a small Colt from the company's inexpensive lineup. Dubbed the Compact Model, it is a cut-rate Officer's Model. This is a per-

104

sonal gun that I carried for several years. It is absolutely reliable and a good companion. The spring-within-a-spring technology used in this pistol resulted in less felt recoil than any previous compact semiauto pistol in this caliber.

Controls were crisp in action and the trigger quite acceptable. The sights, while not highly developed, are adequate for the job. The finish was the poorest feature. Its matte finish showed wear almost with the first draw, but showed little further degradation after reaching a certain point. This pistol has fired over 3,500 rounds since it was purchased new, without a malfunction of any type. It is a genuine good buy, a first-class concealment pistol. I recommend Metalform six-round magazines over factory Colt magazines. Trigger compression was 6.5 pounds as issued and settled into 5.5 pounds after 1,500 rounds of use.

Previously Fired:	Over 2,000 Rounds	
Controls	G	
Fit and finish	P	
Trigger	G	(6.5 lbs.)
Sights	G	
Sharp Edges	G	
Overall	G	
Malfunctions	One: a failure to cycle with +P	

Signature Groups:
230-grain FMJ handload	5.1 inches
Hornady 230-grain FMJ	4.5 inches
Hansen Group: Hornady FMJ	4.0 inches

Rounds Fired:
Montana Gold 230-grain FMJ/231/809 fps	150
Montana Gold 230-grain JHP/321/851 fps	100
Hornady 230-grain FMJ	100
Hornady 185-grain XTP JHP	100
Remington 185-grain +P	50

SPRINGFIELD V 10 1911A1

The V 10 is a compact pistol of pleasing dimensions. The controls were fine, with a little stiffness in the safety. The trigger was heavy, but that is to be expected from a mass-produced 1911. The pistol featured a two-tone finish, blue over natural, and hand-filling Hogue pebble-grain grips. The grips cannot be overrated; Springfield is wise to fit pistols with these grips. The sights were better than those on the Colt 1991A1, if not quite up to the standards of the Kimber, but the V 10 cost less than the Kimber.

The promise of the V 10 is recoil control. The pistol features a line of ports near the muzzle that significantly reduce muzzle flip. The problem with such devices is that they prevent firing the weapon from low ready or eye level because the gas and bullet fragments from the ports will invade your eyes with disastrous results. There is some velocity loss, but not severe. Finally, the muzzle blast is overpowering. When firing the weapon with heavy hearing protection, the difference in muzzle blast was noticeable. Blast was felt on the face. I would not want to fire this handgun without hearing protection.

While the felt recoil was indeed lighter than that of any other compact pistol tested, I did not enjoy firing the pistol due to the blast from the muzzle ports, and the muzzle blast was definitely a factor in controlling the handgun. Some of our test shooters reported less of a problem and commented on the ease of control when firing this pistol. The hotter the load, the more noticeable was the muzzle flip reduction. All in all, the V 10 is a well-made, reliable handgun that should prove a good choice for those favoring ported handguns. As for myself, I would feel quite comfortable with the gun after replacing the barrel with a model without ports! This pistol fit my hand much better than the high-capacity frame Springfields.

Previously Fired:	New Gun	
Controls	F	
Fit and Finish	G	
Sights	G	
Trigger	G	(6.0 lbs.)
Sharp Edges	G	
Overall	G	
Malfunctions	0	

Signature Groups:	
Black Hills FMJ	4.4 inches
Cor-Bon 165-grain JHP	4.6 inches
Speer 230-gr Gold Dot	3.8 inches
Hansen Group:	3.8 inches
Rounds Fired:	
Black Hills 230-grain FMJ	100
Sierra 230-grain FMJ/Unique/756 fps	300
Cor-Bon 165-grain +P	50
Speer 230-grain Gold Dot	50

(I avoided lead bullets due to the possibility of heavy residue buildup in the ports.)

SPRINGFIELD WIDE-BODY COMPACT

This is simply the compact pistol with a high-capacity magazine. Holding 10 rounds of .45 ACP ammunition, this fat little magazine brings with it a penalty. The grip frame becomes a stretch for my average size hands. This pistol was put together by my friends at Dixie Shooter and as a result is quite smooth in operation, with good trigger action. The work cannot be faulted. The pistol worked well, but I found myself hampered in full-speed drills by the wide frame. Still, with some practice I was able to access the pistol from the Milt Sparks Summer Special holster with a degree of speed. The pistol is mild mannered, accurate, and reliable. I have to admit the tuned trigger made the pistol much easier to use well. The gun offers good magazine capacity, which translates to a reserve of ammunition and passing fair accuracy.

Previously Fired:	Perhaps 100 Rounds.	
Borrowed Gun	Fired 100 Rounds	
Controls	G	
Fit and finish	G	
Sights	G	
Trigger	E	(Less than 4 lbs.)
Sharp Edges	F	
Overall	G	

Signature Group:
    Hornady 185-grain XTP   4.0 inches
Hansen Group: 4.5 inches
Rounds Fired:
    Hornady 185-grain XTP   100 rounds

SPRINGFIELD COMPACT/PORTED

This is the same type as the previous example, with two differences. The pistols featured a ported slide/barrel configuration and adjustable sights. I was prepared to like the sights but not the porting. I was correct on both counts. This is another pistol from Dixie shooter and has a nice trigger action. However, I did not like one trait found in some Springfield pistols with the strong firing pin safety. The firing pin stuck forward after dry fire, and I chose not to continue lest the problem rear its head during firing. It was not the fault of the shop; this was a factory defect. The heavy firing pin spring used for safety in some modern pistols will do this. Dixie has corrected the same problem for me in another pistol, and when finished this pistol will work properly. This was not a problem in firing but I did not like this fault.

Previously Fired:	Perhaps a Dozen Rounds	
Controls	G	
Fit and Finish	G	
Trigger	E	(4.0 lbs.)
Sights	G	
Sharp Edges	F	
Overall	G	

Signature Group:
    Hornady 185-grain XTP 100   4.0 inches
Hansen Group: 3.9 inches
Rounds Fired:
    Hornady 185-grain XTP   100 rounds

SPRINGFIELD CHAMPION, STAINLESS STEEL

This is a pistol that uses the short officer's-model-type slide on the full-size frame. As such, it offers a good firing grip and a good, sharp draw. It is fast into action and fast on the target. The plague of these guns is short slide difficulty and the Champion exhibited this fault with lightweight bullets. However, with 230-grain loads, which it liked, it ran smooth. The pistol was very well put together. It had one fault. The edges of the tang and grip safety were so sharp that firing was downright painful. I had to resort to thick Uncle Mike's gloves when firing this gun, but it still gave me a sharp nudge. I corrected the problem with careful polishing and filing, but it was time consuming and painstaking. The first half of the test, fired with the gun as issued, was a daunting experience! I first wrote up a gun of this type for the old *Guns & Gear,* in 1995, and borrowed this example from a new 1911 owner. All have performed well.

Previously Fired:	**500 +**
Controls	**G**
Fit and Finish	**E (Despite sharp edges, a flawless gun)**
Sights	**G**
Trigger	**G** **(5.0 lbs.)**
Sharp Edges	**P**
Overall	**G**

Malfunctions: *8 — Six failures to fully cycle with 185-grain loads. Two slide lock during firing string malfunctions, due to heavy recoil of +P loads.*

Signature Groups
Speer Lawman 230-grain	4.5 inches
Remington 185-grain JHP	5.0

Hansen Group: Cor-Bon +P   5.0 inches

Rounds Fired:
Speer Lawman 230-grain	200 rounds
MagTech 230-grain	200 rounds
Remington 185-grain JHP	50 rounds
Cor-Bon 185-grain +P	50 rounds

SPRINGFIELD CHAMPION

This is the only pistol of this type I have seen. It is the short slide Champion, but in blue finish. The finish is an inexpensive matte blue. This gun was selling for around $325 retail at the time of purchase. Frankly, I did not expect much. The price is low, the gun is meant to sell. But it performed well, better than the much better finished stainless pistol. It fed, chambered, fired, and ejected every cartridge it was fed. Accuracy was OK and the pistol was devoid of sharp edges. Here was a sleeper. I have seen very few for sale and none in the past three years.

Controls	**F**
Fit and Finish	**P**
Trigger	**F** **(6.0 lbs.)**
Sights	**F**
Sharp Edges	**F**
Overall	**G**
Malfunctions	**0**

Signature Groups:
XTP Handload	4.5 inches
Remington UMC	4.0 inches

Hansen Group: Remington 185-grain +P   3.9 inches

Rounds Fired:
Hornady 200-grain XTP/Unique/1,000 fps	100 rounds
Hornady 185-grain XTP/Unique/1100 fps +P	100 rounds
Leadhead 200-grain RNL/Bullseye/801 fps	200 rounds
(Leadhead is a high-quality lead bullet)	
Remington UMC ball	50 rounds
Remington 185-grain JHP +P	50 rounds

PARA ORDNANCE LDA 7.45

This is an Officer's Model LDA pistol in simple terms but a stunningly well-wrought pistol in others. The trigger is something I am not yet used to, but the gun's operation is very smooth. It is very well made, with excellent fit and finish. The only problem experienced during the tests was a failure to feed the last round from the issue seven-round magazine. It is

asking a lot of this magazine to feed from full compression and then feed the last round at almost no compression. I replaced the magazine in further testing with a six-round Metalform magazine, with excellent results.

The signature groups represent my best efforts, but the pistol is far more accurate than I could hold. A few three-round groups fit into a handy inch. This is an outstanding value. I find the LDA system far more attractive in such a light, handy package. With practice this pistol would be a practical service gun on the hip of a supervisor or anyone carrying a great deal of weight on the belt. To qualify both the pistol and the LDA system we worked the gun into several firing sessions, firing a total of 1,000 rounds. Other than a handful of last-round failures to feed with the issue magazine, there were no malfunctions. In other words there were no malfunctions attributable to the pistol or its design.

After a thorough cleaning much later in the test program, we fired the gun again for reliability and overall combat effectiveness. In this case, I had on hand several new magazines from W C Wolff. This reputable firm is breaking into the magazine market. From the experience in this test, the magazines are very good ones. We also wanted to test a new ammunition company, Lancer, that offers good, accurate semi-wad-cutter ammunition, among other types. This took nerve, testing the gun with unproven ammunition and magazines. Naturally, had there been failures I would have had to begin anew. But the gun, magazines, and ammunition passed the test.

Previously Fired:	New Gun	
Controls	E	
Fit and Finish	E	
Trigger	E	(6.0 lbs.)
Sights	E	
Sharp Edges	E	
Overall	E	

Signature Groups:		
Remington UMC		4.5 inches
Cor-Bon 185		3.8 inches
Hansen Group:	Black Hills 185-grain JHP	4.25 inches
Rounds Fired:		
Remington UMC 230-grain		300 rounds
Black Hills 185-grain JHP		100 rounds
Cor Bon 185-grain JHP +P		100 rounds
Second 500 Rounds:		
Remington 230-grain UMC		150 rounds
Lancer 200-grain SWC		300 rounds
Pro Load 200-grain JHP		50 rounds

FIRESTORM

This is one of the best 1911 values on the market. This pistol is different from the 1911 template in many ways. It is a full-size pistol with a short slide, not a true short-dust-cover Commander type. The slide features an internal extractor, which is generally more rugged but is also made up of more parts. The plunger tube assembly is not staked on, but screwed on, which should be an improvement.

The pistol will not take standard 1911 grips. The issue rubber grips are fine, but this is not a gun you will be able to fit with custom grips. The trigger operation is different from most 1911s, with an action bar running from the trigger. The finish is only fair, and showed premature wear. The front sight was nearly worn off after 500 presentations from the holster, indicating soft steel. But what the pistol did was work. This gun has gone on to fire over 1,000 rounds without a malfunction or misfire of any type. I don't know how long it will last compared with a Colt, but the chances are it will not compare favorably in long-term use, but if test-fired and kept at ready in a drawer or in the office, it will do the work of a .45 for those who are on a strict budget. I lubricated it properly, cleaned it every 500 rounds, and it works. The beavertail is long enough to keep the gun comfortable, and it takes Colt magazines. No, this is not the gun I will show off to visiting dignitaries, but it works on demand.

Previously Fired:	New Gun	
Controls	F	
Fit and Finish	F	
Trigger	G	(4.9 lbs.)
Sights	P	
Sharp Edges	G	
Overall	G	

Signature Groups:
CCI Blazer		5.0 inches
Remington 185-grain JHP		4.4 inches
Hansen Group:	CCI Blazer	3.2 inches

Rounds Fired:
CCI Blazer	300 rounds
Remington 185-grain JHP	100 rounds
Speer 230-grain TMJ/231/	50 rounds
Cor-Bon 200-grain JHP +P	50 rounds

ACCURATE PLATING & WEAPONRY COMMANDER

This pistol is a1991A1 cut-rate version of the Commander. It is a steel frame gun with good handling. I tested just such a pistol, in stock form, for this book. They are solid bargains and I recommend them. The Accurate Plating & Weaponry pistol is what happens when you turn a top pistolsmith like Bob Cogan loose on a pistol. The trigger action was finished at a beautiful, crisp three pounds. It actually settled in just a little lighter after some use. The sights were not changed: the standard 1991A1 sights were drilled and enameled in three dots. The ejection port was lowered and polished, a Clark full-length guide rod and Smith & Wesson beavertail safety were added, and the feed ramp and chamber were polished. The pistol was hard-chromed for genuine hard use. This, of course, is Cogan's specialty and his hard chrome and refinish of all types are second to none.

Frankly, the pistol should not have shot as well as it did, but the trigger action, grip safety and simple sight improvement added up to more than the sum of its parts. Here was a pistol that performed very well on small targets at moderate range. The pistol shot as well as any of the five-inch-barrel guns tested, which was surprising. This is one of those wonder guns that we occasionally run across. I have been a skeptic of full-length guide rods, but in this case the rod just may have something to do with the pistol's sterling accuracy. This is a great all-around defense and carry handgun, the Commander size gun at its best. I still prefer Government Model-length guns and this pistol was something of an experiment. If all Commanders were like this one I would have no need for any other pistol.

Previously Fired:	Less than 200 Rounds before Modification.	
Before test:	at least 1,000 rounds	
Controls	G	
Fit and Finish	E	
Trigger	E+	(3.0 lbs.)
Sights	G	
Sharp Edges	E	
Overall	E	

Signature Groups:		
Remington 185-grain JHP		2.25 inches
Remington 185-grain +P		2.0 inches
Hansen Group:	MagTech	2.5 inches
Remington +P		3.0 inches
Rounds Fired:		
Remington 185-grain JHP		100
Remington 185-grain JHP +P		100
Sierra 230-grain FMJ/Titegroup 845 fps		250
MagTech 230-grain ball		50

COLT COMPACT 1991A1

Colt calls this its cut-grade 1911. It is a Commander by any other name. The trigger and mainspring housing are plastic but the sights are steel; the gun features a large ejection port, and the sights, while not true custom high-visibility sights, are larger than those found on the 1911A1 military pistol. The first 1991 Compact I owned was fired a couple hundred times and sent to Accurate Plating & Weaponry for a custom job. I thought it behooved us to test a gun similar to the one I first tested at Guns & Gear over 10 years ago.

This gun is a pre-Keyes gun, and is fitted with the cheapest stocks ever seen on a Colt — made of hard plastic. The pistol's controls were OK in operation, neither crisp nor loose. Trigger compression was acceptable with just a trace of creep and some backlash. When we began shooting the pistol, it looked better. There were no malfunctions and the pistol was very quick on target. The finish was a problem. After fewer than a dozen draws from concealment, the thumb-break of our holster made an unpleasant mar on the pistol's finish. The grips cracked after 450 rounds. Newer 1991s are fitted with rubber grips, an improvement. These grips did not support the plunger tube. I fitted a set of smooth Hogue grips and enjoyed good results. Overall, I like this gun. It is an affordable, reliable pistol with many good traits. The heavy trigger is perhaps best for a beginner's gun and no detriment in a short-range defense situation. The pistol is acceptable, but it needs a set of grips in this vintage.

Previously Fired:	New Gun	
Controls	G	
Fit and Finish	P	(6.5 lbs.)
Sights	F	
Trigger	P	
Sharp Edges	F	
Overall	G	

Signature Groups:		
Federal Hydra Shock		4.8
Hansen Group:	Federal Hydra Shock	4.25 inches
Rounds Fired:		
Remington UMC		200
Remington 230-grain subsonic		50
Fiocchi 230-grain ball		100
Federal Hydra shock		50
West Coat 230-grain plated		100

COLT STAINLESS COMBAT COMMANDER / ENHANCED MODEL

I was prepared to like this pistol a lot, but it left me rather uninterested. The stainless finish showed several brush marks, and the trigger was quite heavy. The enhanced model features were welcome, but the pistol did not perform appreciably better than the 1991A1 — less well in terms of reliability. This is a pre-Keyes gun, and the new president has demanded a tightening of quality. Still, this is a typical 1911, with some fine examples and some mediocre. This particular pistol was OK but could have benefited from a little attention to detail from the maker. The plain rubber grips that covered the front strap of the pistol were not a welcome addition as they stretched the grip frame. I replaced these with beautiful figured grips from Karl Nill. I experienced several failures to cycle with 185-grain ammunition and ultimately replaced the recoil spring with a W C Wolff unit to ensure function. When I owned this pistol I was a working peace officer and eventually traded it for a full-size 1911.

Previously Fired:	New Gun	
Controls	G	
Fit and Finish	P	
Trigger	P	(7.0 lbs)
Sights	G	
Sharp Edges	G	
Overall	G	

Malfunctions: *7 — 4 break-in malfunctions with hardball. No more after break-in period. Slide failed to fully close in first 100 rounds four times — 2, when held at a downward angle and fired; the slide stop locked the pistol to the rear in recoil twice, each time with Cor-Bon 185-grain JHP. The pistol failed once to completely chamber a 185-grain Speer Gold Dot bullet, which was seated with a rap to the rear of the slide. This pistol is at its best with 230-grain loads.*

Signature groups:

Speer Gold Dot 185	3.5 inches
Remington 230-grain FMJ	3.6 inches
Hansen Group: Cor-Bon +P	4.5 inches

Rounds Fired:

Speer 185-grain Gold Dot	50
Speer 230-grain Gold Dot	50
Remington 230-grain FMJ	300
Cor-Bon 185-grain +P	50
Pro Load 230-grain JHP	50
Colt Commander, Series	80

COLT COMMANDER, SERIES 80 BLUE

This was a good solid gun that had seen hard use. I fitted a King's grip safety and speed safety to this pistol. It was clearly a workhorse pistol that had given its owner, a police sergeant, good service. It is among a few of the pistols illustrated that has been bloodied in combat. I did the work for my friend on

fitting the parts, and he tells me he now enjoys firing the pistol much, much more than before. The previous grip safety often produced a welt in the web of his hand. He also reports that the safety is not only quicker to disengage but much handier to activate in the "on" position. When I asked to fire the gun for this report as an example of the Series 80, he simply shrugged. He knew 500 rounds would not hurt the gun and would be good practice. I fired the signature groups; my gang fired the rest. This gun is completely reliable. It is fitted with King's Hardballer Sights, a considerable improvement over the issue sights, but it is basically stock. The feed ramp has never been touched, but this pistol fed anything.

Previously Fired:	Estimated 5,000 rounds	
Controls	E	
Fit and Finish	G	
Trigger	G	(5.0 lbs.)
Sights	G	
Sharp Edges	F	
Overall	G	

Signature Groups:

WW Handload 230-grain	2.75 inches
WW Handload 230-grain #2	3.5 inches
Hansen Group: Handload #2	3.0 inches

Rounds Fired:

Winchester 230-grain Ball /231/770 fps	100
Winchester 230-grain Ball/ 231/ 845 fps	100
Remington Subsonic 230-grain JHP	100
Oregon Trail 200-grain SWC /Titegroup/890 fps	100
Triton 165-grain Quik Shok +P	50
Triton 185-grain JHP	50

COLT STAINLESS SERIES 80 COMMANDER — KEYES GUN

This is one of the newest guns tested, hot off the assembly line. The new CEO of Colt, Colonel Keyes, is demanding higher quality and a better finish. He has succeeded in his wishes. This Colt became my personal number one carry gun, based on flawless performance and personal taste. Some pistols were more accurate, but this gun is very fast on target and simply looks right and suits my style. It is lively in the hand, transverses quickly between targets, and is controllable in rapid fire. I have done a trigger job, reducing the original six-pound trigger to three and one half pounds. What I have not touched is the feed ramp, springs, and other parts that make the gun reliable. We are now at 4,000 rounds without malfunction. Because this is a long-term test gun, I included the 1,500 rounds the gun had fired before the test and added the 500 during the test. The gun was cleaned and lubricated every 500 rounds and the firing was done in four sessions.

Controls	G	
Fit and Finish	E	
Trigger	G	(6.0 lbs, as issued)
Sights	G	
Sharp Edges	G	
Overall	G	

Malfunctions: *0—2,000-round test program.*

Signature Groups:

Winchester ball load	3.0 inches
Winchester JHP Load	2.9 inches
Hansen Group: Cor-Bon 185-grain JHP	4.0 inches

Rounds Fired:

Winchester 230-grain FMJ/Titegroup/801 fps	300
Winchester 230-grain Ball/Unique/ 920 fps +P	100
Winchester 230-grain JHP/Titegroup/809 fps	100
Winchester 230-grain JHP/Titgroup/867 fps	100
Sierra 185-grain JHP/Universal 1,041 fps	200
Pro Load 230-grain ball	200
MagTech 230-grain ball	250
Speer Lawman 230-grain ball	150
Fiocchi 230-grain ball	100
MagTech 185-grain JHP	150
Fiocchi 200-grain JHP	50
Pro Load 185-grain JHP	50
Pro Load 200-grain JHP	50
Pro Load 230-grain JHP	50
Speer 185-grain JHP	50
Cor-Bon 230-grain JHP	100

COLT COMBAT COMMANDER SATIN NICKEL

This is a very nice original Series 70 pistol. The owner had this pistol stored for years, but elected to begin carrying it and offered it up for the gun-testing program to confirm its reliability. It was universally liked until we fired it. The tang and grip safety were very sharp, making firing the

gun difficult, even painful. It was even sharper than the Springfield Champion that gave us such a difficult time. We put on the Uncle Mike's gloves and commenced to fire the gun in strings of 50 for each tester. The gun worked well but showed us why we were so quick to modify old-model Colts. The bench-rest shooting was a rough job! They would not feed most modern JHPs from the magazine to the chamber so we did not fire them. This was not a surprise; the gun would need a throating job or feed-ramp polish. Just the same, it fed the Remington JHP, which has a good reputation for feeding in old model guns.

Previously Fired:	Unknown, but Few	
Controls	G	
Fit and Finish	E	
Trigger	F	(6.5 lbs.)
Sights	P	
Sharp Edges	P	
Overall	F	

Malfunctions: *6 — all failures to fully chamber steel-cased Wolf ammunition.*

Signature Groups:

Sierra/Titegroup	4.0 inches
Wolff 230-grain ball	4.6 inches

Rounds Fired:

Sierra 230-grain FMJ/Titegroup/850 fps	300
Wolff 230-grain BallHP +P	50

CHARLES DALY .45

This is another 1911 with a full-size frame and a short slide, a popular variation of the .45. This seems to be a popular rendition on the theme. The Charles Daly has reasonably good sights that are dovetailed in the

front, and a good beavertail. It has good features for the modest price. We experienced some difficulty with extraction of spent cases, a total of 34 malfunctions in firing the first 250 rounds. I tried to adjust the extractor with my Weigand tool and re-cut the extractor as well. Performance was improved, but overall not 100 percent with all loads, since we experienced a further 11 malfunctions for a total of 45 malfunctions in the 500 rounds fired. This is disturbing, as even Remington cases were involved, and Remington has a reputation for feeding when nothing else will.

The extractor was not the same as in the Colt

1911; it is shorter, and could not be replaced by an Ed Brown or Wilson unit. KBI offered to repair the gun for free, even though I was not the original owner, which speaks well of their customer service.

Previously Fired:	Unknown, used gun	
Controls	F	
Fit and Finish	F	
Sights	F	
Trigger	F	(7.0 lbs.)
Sharp Edges	F	
Overall	F	

Signature Groups:

Wolff 230-grain ball	3.9 inches	
Remington 230-grain JHP subsonic	3.6 inches	
Hansen Group: Wolff ball	5.0 inches	

Rounds Fired:

Wolff 230-grain ball	100	(17 failures to extract)
Blazer 230-grain ball	200	(16 failures to extract)
Remington 230-grain JHP subsonic	100	(7 failures to extract)
Winchester 185-grain Silvertip	50	(4 failures to extract)
MagTech 185-grain JHP	50	(1 failure to extract)

CHARLES DALY #2

I elected to try another Charles Daly and was able to find a similar pistol at a later date. I had fitted the first with grips from Esmeralda O'Sheehan; the second gun was fitted with light-color Smith and Alexander grips. The plastic factory grips leave much to be desired. The second gun was a better performer than the first. In fact, I sometimes carried the gun on administrative and courtroom duty.

Controls	F	
Fit and Finish	F	
Trigger	G	(5.0 lbs.)
Sights	G	
Sharp Edges	P	
Overall	G	

Signature Group:

Lawman ball	4.5 inches
Hansen Group: Remington Golden Saber,	5.0 inches

Rounds Fired

Lawman ball	50
Remington Golden Saber 185 JHP	50
Fiocchi 230-grain ball	200
Wolff 230-grain ball	200

Malfunctions: *2 failures to fully cycle with 185-grain loads.*

GOVERNMENT-LENGTH PISTOLS

COLT SERIES 70

This pistol was in fine shape for its age. Originally finished in nickel, the pistol showed much surface wear but none on the internal workings. It had been handled more than fired. Notably, the feed ramp and collet bushing were spotless. The fit of all parts was first-class, and the trigger was a smooth five pounds. The sights are on the small side, but the gun handled well. The arched mainspring housing and short trigger are ideal for most hands.

The pistol was more accurate than it should have been, giving excellent results. And, best of all, the pistol fed hollow-points well, which many Series 70s do not. (I had one that fed even the notorious 200-grain Speer JHP, but it beat the noses up on feeding.) Modify this gun or keep it original? Well, the finish is not perfect. It would make a very nice carry gun with the simple addition of King's sights. I did have difficulty in seeing the sights in the indoor range we used for this portion of the test program.

Previously Fired:	Unknown	
Controls	G	
Fit and Finish	G	
Trigger	E	(5.0 lbs.)
Sights	P	
Sharp Edges	F	
Overall	G	

Signature Groups:	
Black Hills 185-grain JHP	3.0
Black Hills 230-grain JHP	3.25
Hansen Group: Black Hills 185-grain JHP	3.0
Rounds Fired:	
Black Hills 185-grain JHP	100
Black Hills 230-grain JHP	100
Stars 200-grain SWC/321/1,000 fps	100
Mastercast 200-grain XTP load	100
CCI Blazer	100

SERIES 80, STAINLESS COLT

This pistol followed the Series 70 in production. The Series 80 is a better gun. I know that some shooters lamented the addition of a firing pin safety and its supposed adverse effect on reliability and trigger action, but this supposed fault has not revealed itself in service. The Series 80 has better sights than any previous Colt, the finish is good, and the pistols usually feed any type of hollow-point. I have found that the stainless guns need a longer break-in at times and should be lubricated often, but they give excellent service. The Series 80 Colt is a very good choice, and anyone with this type of pistol is well armed indeed. The stainless pistols are usually the best performers.

Previously Fired:	**Over 3,000**	
Controls	E	
Fit and Finish	G	
Trigger	G	(5.5 lbs.)
Sights	G	
Sharp Edges	F	
Overall	G	

Signature Groups:

Federal 230-grain Hydra Shock	3.5 inches
Winchester 230-grain SXT	3.2 inches
Hansen Group: Wolff ball	3.4 inches

Rounds Fired:

Wolff 230-grain ball	350
Federal 230-grain Hydra Shock	50
Winchester SXT +P	50
Winchester SXT 230-grain	50

COLT ENHANCED-MODEL STAINLESS

This pistol was among the most quietly capable tested. It was a long-term test pistol at my police agency and served well. The grips that covered the front strap were a stretch for some hand sizes, but usable. The sights are better than the military issue and, if not ideal, are the equal of the other service pistols, such as the SIG, and quite superior to the blocky Glock sight. The trigger was good. This pistol eventually went 15,000 rounds without any trouble at all. The finish seemed a little rough, but then, a service gun does not have to be pretty. This is a good, solid pistol. I recorded rounds fired carefully at the PD, but many of them were on my own time. The gun was lubricated with Birchwood Casey gun oil every 500 rounds and cleaned at 1,000 rounds. It never failed and did not require a break-in.

Previously Fired:	**0**	
Controls	G	
Fit and Finish	F	
Trigger	G	(6.0 lbs.)
Sights	G	
Sharp Edges	F	
Overall	G	

Signature Groups:

Winchester 230-grain ball	4.0 inches
Winchester SXT	3.0 inches
Winchester SXT +P	3.25 inches
Hansen Group: not executed during this test program	

Rounds Fired:

Winchester USA 230-grain ball	500
Winchester 230-grain SXT	300
Winchester 230-grain SXT +P	200
Remington 230-grain Golden Saber	100
Federal 230-grain Hydra Shock	100
Federal 185-grain JHP	50

Hornady 230-grain XTP +P	50
Federal 185-grain Hydra Shock +P	100
Speer 200-grain Gold Dot +P	100

I experienced sluggish feeding as the round count neared 1,500 rounds and the pistol had not been cleaned. I cleaned and lubricated the Colt and it ran again for over 1,000 rounds without cleaning. This was a reliable weapon! This Enhanced Model shared the features of the long-term test gun in service at my PD. However, it was delivered with grips similar to the other gun, but they were smooth instead of textured. It was a serviceable gun, but those grips were the cheapest, worst-feeling grips I have ever held. Still, this gun became a personal weapon and served well enough. The beveled magazine well and slightly enlarged controls were a welcome improvement over the standard Series 80.

COLT ENHANCED-MODEL STAINLESS (2)

Controls	F	
Fit and Finish	G	
Trigger	P	(7.0 lbs.)
Sights	G	
Sharp Edges	F	
Overall	G	

Signature Groups:

Winchester 230-grain Black Talon	4.0 inches
Federal 185-grain JHP	3.9 inches
Hansen Group: Federal 185-grain JHP	4.0 inches

Rounds Fired:

Winchester USA ball	400
Federal 185-grain JHP	50
Winchester 230-grain Black Talon	50

COLT 1991A1

When I first saw the 1991A1 pistols, I was convinced of two things. First, the pistols were an answer to competition from Springfield. Second, they were ugly. But then, aren't all 1911s rather blocky, and don't we call them "Old Ugly"? In any case, this is a gun made to sell for less than the Enhanced Model. It uses a composite trigger and mainspring housing, but

so does the Enhanced Model. The pistols feed hollow-points well, have a large ejection port, and good if not outstanding sights. The trigger action is usually good. Money is saved in hand finishing, and the finish is not the pistol's strong suit. The stainless versions are good buys. They are as rugged as any 1911 in my experience. The pistol has a long trigger and flat mainspring housing, which I do not particularly care for. This pistol is quite reliable and should serve as well as any stock 1911. Mine proved completely reliable. Because this is an important pistol in the Colt lineup, we tested it to 1,000 rounds.

Previously Fired	New Gun	
Controls	G	
Fit and Finish	G	
Trigger	G	(4.5 lbs.)
Sights	G	
Sharp Edges	G	
Overall	G	

Signature Groups:

Sierra 230/231	3.4
Wolff 230-grain	4.5
Hansen Group: Wolff 230-grain	4.0

Rounds Fired:

Sierra 230-grain FMJ/231/876 fps	400
Wolff 230-grain ball	100
Blazer 230-grain ball	200
Winchester 185-grain Silvertip	100
Black Hills 185-grain JHP	100
Triton 165-grain Quik Shok +P	100

Malfunctions: *a breakage, the only one during the tests despite the gun's good performance. The cheap plastic grips cracked! This was common in the 1991A1, and modern pistols have rubberized grips.*

COLT 1991A1 IMPROVED

I fitted a stainless steel trigger, slide stop, and slide lock safety from Brownell's to this personal pistol. But two improvements counted for the most. I reduced the trigger compression to a safe, usable 3.0 pounds and fitted a set of IWI night sights. The result is a reliable, usable pistol that did not require that the owner mortgage the ranch. It turned out very well. We capped the job off with a beautiful set of Hogue finger-groove grips. This pistol is now on duty in the South as a peace officer's personal handgun.

Previously Fired:	Unknown, Purchased Used	
Controls	E	
Fit and Finish	G	
Trigger	E	(3.0 lbs.)
Sights	G	
Sharp Edges	E	
(Turned out with a good smooth finish from Colt)		
Overall	G	

Signature Groups:

Star 200-grain SWC		3.0 inches
Federal 230-grain MATCH		2.5 inches
Hansen Group:	Star 230-grain RNL	4.0 inches

Rounds Fired:

Star 200-grain SWC/Titegroup/860 fps	300
Star 230-grain RNL/Titegroup/867 fps	100
Federal 230-grain MATCH	50
Cor-Bon 185-grain +P	50

BEARCOAT ENHANCED MODEL

This is my long-term service handgun. It fired well over 15,000 rounds in its service life. At 11,500 rounds the plunger tube assembly failed. The slide lock broke soon after. With replacement parts, the gun worked — and it never stopped functioning. The gun was a stock Stainless Enhanced Model that was upgraded by Rocky Mountain Arms and Dixie Shooter. Dixie replaced the long trigger with a GI model and adjusted it to 3.0 pounds. This was

done when the gun had fewer than 500 rounds through it — the trigger never failed or went out of adjustment. I fitted a Wilson Grip safety, which I needed because I sometimes missed the safety in high-speed drills. I also specified a set of IWI night sights. At about 13,000 rounds the front sight insert came out. Finally, I added Wilson Combat grips in the gun's last days of service. The final touch was Bearcoat. This Teflon-based finish is resistant, practically immune in fact, to corrosion. It is also self-lubricating. The pistol never needs oiling — it only needs to be kept clean. It is far easier to clean than any other 1911 tested. There were no malfunctions of any kind with this pistol in its service life, only the breakages caused by long, hard use. Based on this experience, and that with the other stainless Enhanced Government Models, these are very good weapons, a top choice.

Previously Fired:	**Approximately 16,000 Rounds**	
Controls	G	
Fit and Finish	E	
Trigger	E	**(3.0 lbs., set by Dixie Shooter)**
Sharp Edges	E	
Overall	E	

Signature Groups:
Black Hills 230-grain ball	3.9 inches
Black Hills 230-grain JHP. JHP	3.0 inches
Hansen Group: Winchester 230-grain SXT +P	3.0 inches

Rounds Fired:
Black Hills 230-grain ball	200
Black Hills 230-grain JHP	200
Winchester SXT +P	50
Oregon Trail 200-grain SWC/Titegroup/890 fps	50

BEARCOAT PARTS GUN

This is one of my favorite pistols. It should see more use since it is among the most accurate 1911s I have ever fired. The pistol is made up of parts, the basic components being an Essex frame and slide and Wilson Combat internal parts. I bought the slide used and it came with a no-name Millet-type, high-profile adjustable sight I did not particularly like. The finish is two tone gray and black Bearcoat with its marvelous self-lubricating property. Dixie Shooter gave the gun a very nice 3.0-pound trigger. This is not what one considers a high-end custom gun, it is a simple, personalized gun that works very well and is completely reliable. The grips are a specially picked set from Smith & Alexander.

Previously Fired:	**1,500 Rounds**	
Controls	G	
Fit and Finish	E	

Trigger	E	(3.0 lbs.)
Sights	E	
Sharp Edges	P	(Due to sights)
Overall	E	

Signature Groups:

Mastercast 200-grain XTP	2.9 inches
Winchester 230-grain SXT	3.65 inches
Hansen Group: Mastercast 200-grain XTP	2.9 inches

Rounds Fired:

Winchester 230-grain ball	200
Winchester 230-grain SXT	100
Mastercast 200-grain JHP	100
West Coast 230-grain Plated/W231/799 fps	100

BEARCOAT TWO-TONE

This is more of a fighting than a target pistol. This is the same pistol previously covered, but rebuilt in a different form more than four years later. The bobbed Government Model hammer and Ed Brown beavertail remain, but the pistol now sports rather plain grips and is not as highly developed as the other guns, but it is a good performer. The sights are Wilson Combat pyramid, top-flight sights that give every advantage. The old high-profile sights were trashed. But what makes the pistol truly different is the addition of a Bar Sto Precision barrel. After much thought, I felt that the gun was now different enough to warrant a second test. There are those who say a tightly

fitted barrel and slide are not reliable. We put a lie to that statement. With all due respect to Bearcoat, due to the machining work done, Wilson Combat refinished the slide in Armor Tuff.

Controls	G	
Fit and Finish	E	
Sights	E	
Trigger	G	(3.0 lbs.)
Sharp Edges	E	
Overall	E	

Signature Groups:

MasterCast 200-grain XTP	1.25
Black Hills 185-grain JHP	1.9
Hansen Group: Winchester ball	2.5

Rounds Fired:

Mastercast 200-grain XTP	200
Black Hills 185-grain JHP	100
Winchester USA ball	200

HIGH STANDARD G MAN

This is my personal number one competition gun. The G Man impressed me with its traditional lines and looks. While the original sported a subdued black finish, beautiful walnut grips, and a round top slide, it is thoroughly modern in performance. The trigger was a crisp, clean, and very neat 3.0 pounds and has held this weight in firing thousands of rounds of full-power ammunition. The original sights have been replaced with Wilson Pyramid

night sights, and the grips are now ergonomic Falcon synthetic grips. This weapon fits my hand and personal style. It is a masterpiece of proper fit and mating of all surfaces, and other examples that I have examined are as well. When I first ordered the G Man, I ordered the SFS trigger action to be able to evaluate this concept. It has proven more than acceptable, and, while I prefer the original single action type, it has not stopped the G Man from becoming my primary carry gun. I have taken game and won matches using this gun and it has given me many hours of shooting pleasure. I have included a 2,000 round test to judge the weapon's trigger action — it is not fragile — as well as to demonstrate the overall reliability of this extraordinary pistol. This test program took place over perhaps 18 months.

Previously Fired:	7,500 Rounds Plus	
Controls	E	
Fit and Finish	E	
Trigger	E	(2.9 lbs.)
Sights	E	
Sharp Edges	E	
Overall	E	

Signature Groups:

Federal 230-grain Hydra Shock	2.5 inches
Fiocchi ball	3.4 inches
Mastercast 200-grain	2.0 inches
Hansen Group: Fiocchi ball	3.0 inches

Rounds Fired:

Fiocchi 230 grain ball	500
Fiocchi 200-grain JHP	200
MagTech 185-grain JHP	100
Weber 230-grain ball	500
Remington 185-grain JHP	50
Mastercast 200-grain XTP	100
Federal 230-grain Hydra Shock	50
Oregon Trail 200-grain SWC/Titegroup/890 fps	200

KIMBER .45

I had a late start on the Kimber bandwagon. Kimber is the single largest maker of 1911 pistols and has managed to acquire and maintain an excellent reputation. The pistols are basically high-production custom pistols, fitted from high-quality parts by experienced technicians. The pistols feed all types of ammunition, feature good sights and excellent controls as issued, and usually have good trigger action. I first took notice when tactical expert Denny Hansen gave the Kimber a favorable review in *SWAT* Magazine. That was enough for me — I later learned that, if anything, Mr. Hansen's review was understated. I cannot recall another pistol that gave such brilliant groups, so easily, under two inches off the rest, in 25 years of shooting. My experience with Kimber pistols has been uniformly excellent.

A local 1911 expert and gunsmith, Jim Dunbar, rates the Kimber as the best 1911 he has seen. That is good enough for me and should be good enough for anyone. These two recommendations carry a great deal of weight. Hansen's reputation in the professional community is second to none. It is interesting to note that he has left his combat Tupperware behind these days in favor of the Kimber. Because this is a long-term test gun I am covering for several law enforcement-related publications as well as for the popular press, I was able to devote a disproportionate amount of time to this gun. Also, while doing research for an article on handloading the .45 ACP, this was my test vehicle.

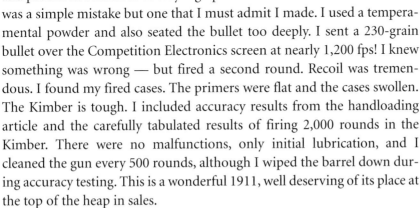

I have to be truthful — I made an error in loading and produced a number of very high pressure rounds. It was a simple mistake but one that I must admit I made. I used a temperamental powder and also seated the bullet too deeply. I sent a 230-grain bullet over the Competition Electronics screen at nearly 1,200 fps! I knew something was wrong — but fired a second round. Recoil was tremendous. I found my fired cases. The primers were flat and the cases swollen. The Kimber is tough. I included accuracy results from the handloading article and the carefully tabulated results of firing 2,000 rounds in the Kimber. There were no malfunctions, only initial lubrication, and I cleaned the gun every 500 rounds, although I wiped the barrel down during accuracy testing. This is a wonderful 1911, well deserving of its place at the top of the heap in sales.

Controls	E	
Fit and Finish	G	**(The finish has shown some nicks and holster wear)**
Sights	E	
Trigger	E+	**(4 lbs.)**
Sharp Edges	G	
Overall	E	

Signature Groups:

Winchester USA ball	3.0 inches
Federal 185-grain +P	2.5 inches
Black Hills 185-grain JHP	2.0 inches
Black Hills 230-grain JHP +P	2.5 inches
Winchester 230-grain SXT +P	2.9 inches
Sierra 230-grain JHP/Titegroup	1.9 inches
Oregon Trail 230-grain RNL/Bullseye	2.0 inches
Oregon Trail 200-grain SWC/Titegroup	1.9 inches
Black Lion 230-grain FP/Titegroup	1.85 inch
Hansen Group: W- 230-grain SXT +P	3.0 inches

Rounds Fired:

Winchester USA ball	50
Federal 185-grain Hydra Shock +P	50
Black Hills 185-grain JHP	50
Black Hills 230-grain JHP	50
Black Hills 230-grain JHP +P	50
Winchester SXT 230-grain +P	50
Sierra 230-grain JHP/Titegroup/855 fps	450
Sierra 230-grain JHP/W231/876 fps	100
Oregon Trail 200-grain SWC/titegroup/899 fps	200
Oregon Trail 230-grain RNL/bullseye/801 fps	200
Black Lion 230-grain /Titegroup/845 fps	100
Hornady 230-grain XTP/Unique/920 fps	100
Hornady 200-grain XTP/Unique/978 fps	100
Star 185-grain SWCHP/Clays/909 fps	300
Weber 230-grain FMJ 850 fps	50

I test-fired 2,000 rounds with fine accuracy. The FBI test ran 25,000 rounds and various agency tests make mine look insignificant, but I was impressed. No malfunctions of any type were suffered and the pistol gave excellent accuracy. It is as tight as ever, with little detectable wear.

SEMICUSTOM KIMBER

This was another stock Kimber in most ways, but with two additions. I added a Wilson Combat grip adaptor that slides on over the front strap. This makes for a front strap that more closely resembles the LAPD SWAT gun. Also, I carefully massaged the mating surfaces of the trigger to bring the trigger compression to a smooth and very clean 3.0 pounds, invalidating an ironclad warranty in the process. This is a very good gun, but not appreciably better than the other, stock Kimber that was tested. I did like the improved front strap, however. With the addition of self-luminous iron sights at a later date, I will have the LAPD SWAT pistol. I can see why Dane Burns has modified so many Kimbers. With a little work, they can be even better pistols. While Grandfather may have had a Colt, the Kimber may be the thinking man's choice.

Previously Fired:	0	
Controls	E	
Fit and Finish	G	
Sights	G	
Trigger	E	(3.0 lbs.)
Sharp Edges	E	
Overall	E	

Signature Groups:

Weber 230-grain ball	3.0 nches
Federal 230-grain MATCH	2.4 inches
Hansen Group: Winchester Ranger Partition Gold	2.5 inches

Rounds Fired:

Weber 230-grain ball	200
West Coat 230-grain Plated/Titegroup/850 fps	100
Federal 230-grain MATCH	100
Winchester 185-grain Partition Gold	50
Black Hills 185-grain JHP	50

SPRINGFIELD LOADED MODEL/STAINLESS STEEL

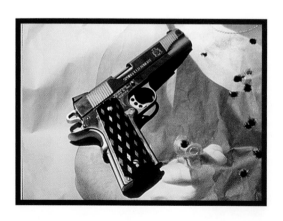

This is another long-term test pistol that I have covered in several popular publications. This is a middle-range Springfield. It is more evolved than the Military Specification pistols, with some examples having extended safeties and beavertails as well as Novak sights. The pistol is found in numerous configurations. Most offer good value, but this particular example offered extraordinary performance. Overall, I have the impression that the stainless steel Springfield pistols are better fitted and perform better than the carbon steel pistols. This may just be an impression, but if so, it is grounded in fact. This pistol was one of the better out-of-the-box 1911s of any type we have tested. Of the three Loaded Models tested, this is my favorite, even though I fitted another with a Nowlin barrel and other custom parts. This pistol simply came out of the box shooting, continued to shoot, and proved to be a gun that liked practically any load it was fed. This is a good personal defense weapon or all-around shooter. We fired this pistol to a full 1,000 rounds in a number of sessions, including several at 50 yards.

Controls	G	
Fit and Finish	E	
Trigger	E	(4.0 lbs.)
Sights	G	
Sharp Edges	G	
Overall	G	

Signature Groups

Sierra 230-grain JHP/920 fps	3.0 inches
Black Hills 230-grain ball	2.5 inches
Hansen Group: Black Hills 230-grain ball	3.25 inches

Rounds Fired:

Sierra 230-grain JHP/Unique/920 fps	100
Black Hills 230-grain RNL	100
Black Hills 200-grain SWC	100
Speer 185-grain Gold Dot	50
Federal 230-grain TACTICAL JHP	50
Federal 185-grain Hydra Shock +P	50
Cor-Bon 185-grain JHP +P	50
Second session: All Mec Gar Magazines	
Phoenix 230-grain RNL/Titegroup/850 fps	250
Hornady XTP 200-grain/Titegroup/890 fps	100
Weber 230-grain ball	100
Black Hills 230-grain JHP +P	50

SPRINGFIELD LOADED MODEL #2

When I received this gun, I found a plain matte-finished pistol with a Novak rear and standard post front sight but with a good beavertail safety. The long trigger was nice enough at five pounds. This pistol featured a flat mainspring housing. I did not like the issue grips and fitted it with a set of Kim Ahrends' tactical or half-checkered grips. This worked out very well indeed, giving good purchase and more than a little eye appeal. In dry fire I found that the firing pin occasionally stuck forward, a problem in some pistols with an over-strength firing pin spring. I changed the spring and eventually had to change the firing pin to cure the prob-

lem. I also adjusted the trigger to a clean, smooth four pounds from the issue six pounds, but did not address slide-to-barrel fit. Overall, the pistol was more than acceptable after a little tweaking. It suffered no malfunctions other than that the rear sight retaining screw worked loose when firing +P ammunition and found its way into my sight picture. This is a fault that we should be aware of in all guns with this type of sight. This pistol was a test device for several types of ammunition and performed well.

Controls	G	
Fit and Finish	G	
Trigger	G	**(6.0 lbs. after adjustment, E for 4 lbs.)**
Sights	G	
Sharp Edges	G	
Overall	G	

Signature Groups:

Weber 230-grain	3.5 inches
Remington 230-grain Golden Saber	3.0 inches

Hansen Group:

Weber 230-grain ball	4.0 inches

Rounds Fired:

Weber 230-grain ball	200
Remington 230-grain Golden Saber	100
Oregon Trail 200-grain SWC/Bullseye/890 fps	100
West Coast 185-grain Plated/Unique/900 fps	50
Triton 185-grain JHP +P	50

SPRINGFIELD LOADED/BUREAU MODEL STANDARD

This pistol began life as a Springfield Loaded Model. This is pretty good in itself, but I made a few additions. The pistol was delivered with Novak sights, front cocking serrations, an extended slide lock safety, and a standard grip safety. But best of all, in my eyes, the pistol featured a standard

short trigger. I was looking to build a Springfield roughly comparable to the Springfield Bureau or Professional Model, the pistol purchased by FBI/HRT-SWAT. This pistol costs perhaps $1,500 or more, and I wanted to bring a solid Springfield as near the Bureau Model as possible. I added a Smith & Alexander Mag Guide and a Wilson Combat Extractor and sear. I had the trigger reworked to a nice 3.0 pounds by Dixie Shooter. I added Herrett checkered stocks.

I am convinced, however, that the greatest single improvement was provided by the addition of a Nowlin custom barrel. Specified by the FBI, this barrel greatly improved the accuracy of this gun. I also used an Alpha Precision blocking tool to tighten the slide-to-frame fit. To make it truly comparable to the Bureau gun, it would need a space-age Teflon-based finish. But I doubt I will do any such thing in the near future. This is a hard-working, credible pistol just as it is. With further slide tightening and tweaking, along with load development, the gun would probably meet the 1.25-inch/25-yard standard imposed upon the Springfield Professional Model by the FBI.

Previously Fired:	**Approximately 1,500 Rounds**	
Controls	F	
Fit and Finish	F	
Trigger	E	**(3.0 lbs.)**
Sights	G	
Sharp Edges	G	
Overall	G	

Signature Groups:

Black Hills 230-grain JHP	1.9 inches
Black Hills 185-grain JHP	2.0 inches

Hansen Group:	Sierra Load, 230-grain	3.0 inches

Rounds Fired:

Sierra 230-grain JHP/Titegroup/855 fps	100
Winchester USA Ball	100
Winchester Win Clean	50
Black Hills 230-grain JHP	100
Black Hills 185-grain JHP	100
Black Hills 230-grain RNL	100
Black Hills 200-grain SWC	100
Hornady 230-grain FP	100
Phoenix 230-grain RNL/Unique/850 fps	150
Speer 200-grain Gold Dot +P	100

PARA ORDNANCE P 14

This is a surprisingly handy pistol, despite its large grip frame, required due to the pistol's 13-round magazine. The short trigger and well-designed grip aid in making the pistol friendly to average-size hands. Much of the good handling qualities of the 1911 are preserved in the P 14. A lot of research has gone into designing a comfortable high-capacity grip frame. I have owned several of these pistols and have found that the average kit gun varies depending upon the skill of the person who puts it together. Production guns are usually very good. I like the round top slide and high-visibility sights. Controls are universally crisp, and the trigger is good.

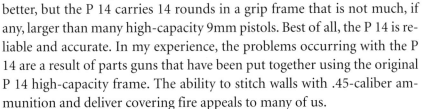

I carried this gun for some time as a peace officer, often wearing it concealed in my Blocker holster, and I can think of no better all-around combat 1911. I am faster with the single-stack 1911, and it fits my hand better, but the P 14 carries 14 rounds in a grip frame that is not much, if any, larger than many high-capacity 9mm pistols. Best of all, the P 14 is reliable and accurate. In my experience, the problems occurring with the P 14 are a result of parts guns that have been put together using the original P 14 high-capacity frame. The ability to stitch walls with .45-caliber ammunition and deliver covering fire appeals to many of us.

Previously Fired:	**Unknown, Purchased Used**	
Controls	G	
Fit and Finish	G	
Trigger	G	(4.5 lbs.)
Sights	G	
Sharp Edges	G	
Overall	G	

Signature Groups:

Speer 200-grain JHP	3.0 inches
Remington 185-grain JHP	3.4 inches

Rounds Fired:

Speer 200-grain JHP	50
(Once a very popular service load, now out of production)	
Federal 230-grain MATCH	150
Winchester Super X 230-grain ball	100
Hornady 185-grain JHP/Herco —1090 fps	100

(This was a pre-XTP, a round-nose JHP that gave good accuracy. The XTP is a better bullet, but I used thousands of these in handloads)

P 14 PARTS GUN WITH MILITARY SLIDE

This pistol consisted of a Para Ordnance frame in fine condition mated to a no-name GI slide and barrel with no marking. I tested it nearly 10 years after I acquired my personal P 14. I didn't expect much, but a friend who wanted to carry the gun asked us to check it out. It turns out that the pistol was well fitted and worked acceptably. It would not feed all JHP ammunition, but with ball ammunition and some hollow-points it was reliable and accurate enough. The small GI sights were typical of the breed. We suspect the worthy who built this gun was disappointed. A good set of sights and more care in fitting would have worked wonders. We tested this gun partly because we have heard bad things about the Para Ordnance kit guns. We found no point in long-term testing of this example, but overall it is interesting. If you go the kit gun route, Para Ordnance has my recommendation. Be sure to choose a Caspian or Essex upper, not a gun show GI slide.

Previously Fired:	Unknown	
Controls	F	
Fit and Finish		
Frame	G	
Slide	P	
Trigger	G	**(6.0 lbs., smooth)**
Sights	P	
Sharp Edges	F	
Overall	G	

Signature Groups:	
Black Hills 230-grain ball	4.75 inches
Hansen Group: Black Hills 230-grain ball	5.0 inches
Rounds Fired:	
Black Hills 230-grain ball	300
Black Hills 200-grain SWC	150
Remington 185-grain JHP +P	50
(Perfect feed reliability)	

PARA ORDNANCE LDA

As covered previously, this is a 1911 with LDA trigger action. This is a full-sized double-column magazine pistol of obvious quality. It is well made, smooth in operation, and reliable. It exhibited a handful of 1911-type break-in malfunctions. Knowing 1911s as I do, and the fact that the malfunctions came in the first 25 rounds and then ceased, this is an encouraging sign. The gun is tight enough for good accuracy but not so tight as to cause malfunctions. This is a new design so we went the extra mile, to a full 1,000 rounds. I squirted a little Birchwood Casey gun oil in the ejection port at 850 rounds, when function seemed sluggish due to accumulated powder ash, but there were no problems after round number 25, even though I fired many lead bullet handloads in this pistol.

This is one to count on. Even if the LDA action is not for you, it should not be discounted. Some shooters are far less likely to clutch the LDA trigger than a single action trigger and may shoot better with this action. The quality of this pistol compared favorably with those in the high-grade-production-pistol class. While my old P 14 is a good pistol, comparable to the Colt, the new Para Ordnance pistols have made great leaps in quality. The P 14 has never malfunctioned and I expect no less from the LDA. While I choose to stick to my single-action pistols, the LDA pistols are good shooters and perhaps a better choice for many shooters.

After getting into the rhythm of this pistol, I find it offers several advantages, especially in home-ready situations. It can be kept hammer-down, safety-on, and ready to fire instantly. I am of the opinion that this would be a fine candidate for a .45 Super conversion — I like this weapon that much. The main difference between this pistol and other 1911s is the trigger. The Light Double Action trigger does not affect the general feel of the 1911. There is no obvious difference in the frame of an LDA gun and a standard single-action. In the forward position the trigger is just slightly longer, requiring a longer reach, than the "long trigger" found

on many modern 1911s. Initial take-up is perhaps three-and-one-half pounds, as the trigger is compressed to the approximate position of a single-action trigger. Then, greater force is required to finish the break, which is usually in the five-and-one-half-to six-and-one-half-pound class. It is smoother than the smoothest double-action revolver, and that is saying a lot. This is a double-action trigger that both cocks the hammer and releases the hammer. The gun cannot be repeatedly cycled, however, in dry fire. In common with the Glock and several other DAO designs, the slide resets the trigger for a following shot. I would not recommend carrying the LDA without the safety on. Unlike many service pistols, which have poorly placed slide-mounted safeties, the LDA's frame-mounted safety is as fast into operation as any other 1911, allowing excellent speed into action. While the hammer rides down with the slide as the gun fires, the hammer does not touch the firing pin. The double-action-only LDA is superior on every count to the Glock and other DAO service guns. This is the number-one first-class DAO service handgun in America. Agencies failing to recognize that fact and continuing to supply their officers with inferior gear do so at their own risk.

Controls	G	
Fit and Finish	E	
Trigger	E	(6.0 lbs.)
Sights	E	
Sharp Edges	E	
Overall	E	

Signature Groups:

Weber 230-grain ball	3.25 inches
Federal 230-grain Hydra Shock	3.5 inches
Powermax 200-grain JHP	3.65 inches

Hansen Group: Weber 230-grain Ball	4.0 inches
Rounds Fired:	
Weber 230-grain ball	350
International Cartridge frangible	200
Lancer 200-grain SWC	200
Phonenix-cast 230-grain RNL/Unique/850 fps	100
Federal 230-grain Hydra Shock	50
Powermax 200-grain Gold Dot +P	100

The gun proved very nice to fire when using +P ammunition. The trigger action aids in preventing flinch or trigger clutch.

WILSON CLOSE QUARTERS BATTLE

Of the pistols tested, this one represented my personal opinion of a highly developed workmanlike custom 1911 better than any other. It is not a full custom gun but one with most of the desirable features a 1911 should have. It worked, and worked with any type of ammunition. The pistol I tested is

not inexpensive, with a price tag hovering near $1,800, but it is well worth the tariff. There are less-expensive Wilson guns and some costing quite a bit more. The pistols performance cannot be faulted. It features well-designed controls, unobtrusive but crisp and positive in action. The sights are excellent, and the factory trigger, set at 3.5 pounds, never failed or fluctuated weight in firing well over 3,500 rounds of ammunition in my test. The first 1,500 rounds were logged in for this book. The pistol features Armor Tuff coating, which makes it nearly impervious to corrosion.

The pistol is better than the comparable pistols I have built with Wilson parts, and it should be. It has Bill Wilson's signature all over it, figuratively speaking. It does not use a full-length guide rod, but a standard recoil spring. This eliminates complication in disassembly and maintenance as well as in administrative handling. If it were fitted a little tighter it might be more accurate, but I have seen more accurate, tightly fitted guns choke during competition. I would not wish to have the compromise. I am certain this pistol would have given excellent groups in a machine rest and was almost tempted to borrow one but demurred, preferring to stay in touch with reality. This is quite a pistol, Bill Wilson's best pistol in my opinion.

Controls	E	
Fit and Finish	E	
Trigger	E +	(3.5 lbs.)
Sights	E	
Sharp Edges	E	
Overall	E (Plus!)	

Signature Groups:	
Sierra 230-grain JHP/920 fps	1.5 inches
Black Hills 230-grain JHP	2.0 inches
Hansen Group: Black Hills ball ammunition	2.5 inches

Rounds Fired:

Black Hills 230-grain JHP	150
Black Hills 185-grain JHP	50
Sierra 230-grain JHP/Unique/920 fps	100
Sierra 230-grain JHP/Titegroup/850 fps	300
Sierra 185-grain JHP/Titegroup/1,050 fps	100
Montana Gold 230FMJ/Titegroup/850 fps	250
Oregon Trail 200-grain SWC/Unique/1,050 fps	100
Black Hills 230-grain JHP +P	100
West Coast 230-grain Plated/Unique/850 fps	350

(An inexpensive bullet compared with jacketed bullet; West Coast bullets gave good results.)

ACTION WORKS

This is a light custom job. Basically, Don Williams elevated an ordinary Colt to Kimber standards. The work cost perhaps $400 and was a bargain. Don fitted a match-grade barrel bushing, completed a reliability package that included a mirror-smooth feedway polish, and adjusted the trigger to a beautiful three pounds let-off. The sights were Novak Lo Mount front and rear, fitted with excellent machine work. I had had some trouble with this pistol. The trigger was rough, and worse, inconsistent. This is among the first Enhanced Models and I did not like it. It simply did not perform as well as other examples tested. It did not feed all hollow-point bullets properly, including the wide-mouth Sierra that was the way to go at the time.

The gun performed much better than expected despite a rather light custom massage. The gun was 100 percent reliable and, like many .45s, this weapon can be surprisingly accurate with loads it likes, and just fair with others. The loads tested represent results from some of the best loads and ammunition available 10 years ago. I think they show quality is consistent. I found that secret sweet spot with this pistol and turned in a number of extraordinary groups. Remember, it had just a factory barrel and nothing else in the way of tightening. I think this gun shows that an average .45 can be a top-notch performer with just a little work, as long as the right man does that work.

Previously Fired:	**About 500, Most of Them Hardball.**	
Controls	E	
Fit and Finish	F	
Trigger	E	(3.0 lbs.)
Sights	F	
Sharp Edges	E	
Overall	E	

Signature Groups:

National Bullet Company 230-grain FP/Unique/855 fps	2.0 inches
Hornady 200-grain JSWC/Bullseye/900 fps	1.5 inches
Speer 200-grain JHP	1.9 inches

Hansen Group: not fired at the time

Rounds Fired:

National Bullet Company 230-grain FP/Unique/850 fps	300
Hornady JSWC/Bullseye/980 fps	100
Surefire 185-grain JHP, 1,134 fps with Hornady XTP bullet	200

There were half dozen break, in malfunctions and several failures to feed JHP ammunition.

This is a far more involved gun. I began with a stainless steel 1991A1. The pistol worked well but was rather ordinary, with a good but ordinary finish. The pistol was bead blasted for smoothness and a better appearance. The trigger action and reliability package done on this gun were most important, but the pistol also received an important addition in the way of sights. A Heinie rear sight and a Novak front were added, as well as a full-length guide rod, and the frame was stippled as well. Last but not least, Don Williams fitted a set of Ahrends grips. The Action Works 1911 is very fast into action, completely reliable, and remarkably easy to use well. Like the earlier pistol, it features Don's trademark drop safety. A neat trick is that the match-grade barrel bushing is only finger tight, allowing ease of field-stripping. You can't buy a gun like this from the factory, but you can have one built.

Controls	E	
Fit and Finish	E	
Trigger	E	(3.0 lbs.)
Sights	E	
Sharp Edges	E	
Overall	E+–	(Shared only with the Wilson Combat Pistol)

Signature Groups:

Winchester 230-grain JHP	2.5 inches
Sierra 230-grain Ball/Bullseye	2.0 inches
Hansen Group: Winchester 230-grain JHP	3.5 inches

Rounds Fired:

Winchester 230-grain JHP (Subsonic)	50
Winchester 185-grain Partition Gold	50
Sierra 230-grain FMJ/Bullseye/850 fps	200
Bull X 230-grain RNL/Unique/800 fps	150
Cor-Bon 185-grain JHP +P	150
Federal 230-grain MATCH	100
Hornady 230-grain ball	100
Hornady 230-grain Flat Point	100
Grindel 185-grain JHP	100

LLAMA WITH CLARK BARREL

This was a nicely blued gun, with the addition of a Clark custom barrel. The trigger has been set to a very nice 2¾ pounds and several surfaces have been jeweled. The owner was on a tight budget but wished to break into IPSC, and this gun gave him much valuable practice and experience. The pistol was purchased new at little cost and he bought the barrel and trigger parts used from a fellow shooter — a good source since IPSC shooters change their pistols around often. It is not possible to change the sights on the Llama, at least not economically. We included this gun as an example of a budget gun and the fact that some of the products turned out by Llama will function adequately. It would not feed hollow-points, — not even the Remington 185-grain JHP — but we got along well with round-nosed handloads.

Controls	P	
Fit and Finish	G	
Trigger	E	(2.75 lbs.)
Sights	P	
Sharp Edges	F	
Overall	P	

Signature Groups:

West Coat RN-plated	2.0 inches
Black Hills ball	3.4 inches
Hansen Group: Black Hills ball	4.0 inches

Rounds Fired:

West Coat 230-grain RNP/231/850 fps	200
Black Hills 230-grain ball	200
Star 200-grain SWC/Accurate #7/1,000 fps	100
(Seven failures to feed SWC)	

LLAMA OLD MODEL

We attempted to test an old-model Llama pistol that we picked up cheaply in a pawnshop, but it refused to function. The Llama sported a nice blue finish and had fair trigger action. While it would feed hollow-points, which was surprising, it failed to extract perhaps half of the rounds fired. The Llama extractor is difficult to remove and repair so we went no further with this gun. There were 27 malfunctions in 60 rounds of ammunition. It did seem to work with hardball ammunition. Like many military or off-brand 1911s, it fed Remington Golden Saber JHP ammunition. It was an unfired, in-the-box gun. Overall, considering that these pistols do not accept standard 1911 parts, I am leery of them. A tightening up of production and a new corporate structure make the new Firestorm far more attractive than any used Llama.

Controls	F	
Fit and Finish	F	
Trigger	F	(5.0 lbs.)
Sights	P	
Sharp Edges	P	
Overall	P	

Signature Groups:

Remington 230-grain Golden Saber	4.6 inches
Hansen Group: Black Hills 230-grain JHP	6.5 inches

Rounds Fired: (Testing stopped at 250 rounds)

Remington Golden Saber	100
Black Hills ball	150

THE HUGHSTON GUN

This pistol exhibited the best trigger of all the guns that we tested. This pistol was built for my old friend T.N. Hughston. It has new production internal parts, including several from Ed Brown's Hard Core line. The frame is Essex and so is the slide. The rear sight is a Bomar fully adjustable sight and

the front, from EGW, is a fiber-optic sight. The barrel and barrel bushing are National Match. This pistol is a classic rendition of the 1911, and a very good one.

Controls	E	
Fit and Finish	G	
Trigger	E+	(4.0 lbs.)
Sights	E	
Sharp Edges	P*	
Overall	E	

Signature Group:

XTP handload	1.5 inches
Gold Dot handload	1.9 inches

Rounds Fired:

XTP/Titegroup 200-grain/880 fps	50
Gold Dot/Titegroup230-grain/790 fps	50

Due to our rating system, geared to combat guns, adjustable sights get poor marks.

CHARLES DALY

This pistol is manufactured in the Philippines as is the Rock Island pistol. The Charles Daly has more refinements. The pistol features good sights and a larger speed safety and grip safety than found on stock 1911-type pistols. These pistols are often good performers. After testing several I would say that some of the parts are not fitted as well as I would like, but, as a beginning 1911, the guns are an attractive option. This version did everything I could ask, and turned in acceptable accuracy.

Controls	G	
Fit and Finish	F	
Trigger	F	(5.5 lbs.)
Sights	G	
Sharp Edges	P	
Overall	G	

Signature Group:

Sellier and Bellot 230-grain ball	3.8 inches
Hansen Group: S and B 230-grain	4.0 inches

Rounds Fired:

Sellier and Bellot ball	200
Winchester 230-grain JHP/231/850 fps	100
Federal Classic 230-grain JHP	100
Oregon Trail 200-grain SWC/Unique/1,050 fps	50
Cor-Bon 165-grain JHP +P	50

JACOBSEN COLT

This pistol was modified by Teddy Jacobsen of Actions by T. The pistol was an original Series 70 Government Model. Teddy enameled the sights in contrasting red and green and did a complete reliability package on this pistol. As a result, the pistol did not malfunction in firing some 15,000 rounds of ammunition. I did break a few parts, however, and that is why it is important to include the results of my longtime use of this pistol. Teddy's action works is renowned in the professional world. He brought the Colt's trigger to a smooth four pounds with no creep or backlash. This action never failed in all of the work that was done with the pistol. This was my competition, hunting, defense, and ammunition test pistol for several years and it was treated to its share of heavy loads.

I worked up a special load for an agent in Alaska who wanted to carry an expanding-bullet load. It had to have excellent penetration, since felons in the northernmost state are often bundled up heavily. We came upon a load using the 250-grain XTP at over 900 fps. Originally designed for the .45 Colt, this bullet would do the business. This pistol would put five into two inches at twenty yards. Unfortunately, at 11,500 rounds the Colt barrel bushing broke. The gun kept going, so I fitted a King's Match grade bushing. At 13,500 rounds the frame cracked just in front of the slide stop. Some 1911s may do this after hard use, especially with very heavy loads. Often, they keep firing and working normally. A friend now has this gun, and while he is aware of its heavy use and the cracked frame, he has fired perhaps 200 rounds a year in the gun for half a decade with good results.

Controls	G	
Fit and Finish	G	
Trigger	E+	(4.0 lbs.)
Sights	G	
Sharp Edges	G	
Overall	E	

Signature Group:	
Federal 230-grain Match	2.0 inches
Hansen Group: Bull XFP	2.9 inches
Rounds Fired:	
Hornady 185-grain JHP Unique/1150 fps	50
Speer 200-grain JHP Unique/1,050 fps	50
Bull XFlatnose 230-grain Unique/950 fps	150
Hornady 250-grain XTP Herco/938 fps	100
RCBS 255-grain SWC Bullseye/947 fps	100
Federal 230-grain MATCH	50
Federal 230-grain MATCH	100
Grindel 185-grain JHP	100
Grindel 230-grain JHP	100
Winchester Silvertip	150
Winchester Super X 230-grain ball	50

AUTO ORDNANCE

This gun probably already had several thousand rounds fired through it when we found it in a pawnshop. Old model AO guns don't sell very well but this one turned out to be a bargain. The controls were mushy but the trigger was very good. The blue finish looked cheesy — a little too shiny and with bad polishing marks. The grips were pebble grain Hogues, a big plus, and the sights were Millett high visibility. The feed ramp appeared to have been polished, and the trigger broke at a light 2.75 pounds. This gun was interesting — I don't know who did the work, but they did it right. The only parts that had received attention were the grip safety and trigger, and perhaps the feed ramp. This .45 was loose, it rattled, and it was not very accurate, but it always worked! The trigger did not follow when the slide was dropped, and it never failed during our test. The grip safety worked well with a definite stage as it engaged the sear. Overall, it was a surprising gun that shows a well-worn 1911 can work well. I would not hesitate to carry this gun — it will do the job.

Previously Fired:	Unknown	
Controls	F	(Mixed: slide stop and safety, P; grip safety, E)
Fit and Finish	P	
Trigger	E	(2.75 lbs.)
Sights	F	
Sharp Edges	F	
Overall	G	

Signature Groups:

Fiocchi 200-grain JHP	4.5 inches
Remington 185-grain JHP +P	4.6 inches
Hansen Group: Remington 185-grain Golden Saber	3.4 inches

Rounds Fired:

Fiocchi 200-grain JHP	100
Remington 185-grain JHP +P	100
Remington 185-grain Golden Saber	50
Speer Flying Ashtray/Unique/200-grain/1,000 fps	200
Speer JHP/Herco 260-grain/780 fps	50

COLT STAINLESS 1991A1

This is yet another Colt, a Keyes production and the next to last gun tested. This test went well and there were no surprises, and in the end the gun's performance neither added nor detracted from the Colt legend. The pistol performed well, as expected, but not spectacularly. It is a good solid gun and circumstances permitted the use of a new entry in the test program — Wayne Novak's magazines. Novak is a respected gunsmith and innovator and his magazines work as expected. Overall, this is a good gun to ride the trail with. The most interesting departure from older 1991A1 guns is that the grips are soft synthetic rubber, much better than the hard rubber grips found on early-model pistols. The gun fed all hollow-points and was overall a good pistol. It is quite usable as is but would be a fine gun to elevate with conservative gunsmithing.

Controls	G	A little stiff, (but worked out with use)
Fit and Finish	E	
Trigger	G	(5.5 lbs.)
Sights	G	
Sharp Edges	F	
Overall	G	

Signature Group:

Sierra 230-grain FMJ/Titegroup	4.0 inches
Winchester 230-grain SXT Ranger	3.5 inches
Hansen Group: Sierra 185-grain JHP loading	4.0 inches

Rounds Fired:

Sierra 230-grain FMJ/Titegroup/850 fps	50
Sierra 230-grain JHP/Titegroup/850 fps	50
Sierra 185-grain SWCFMJ/231/890 fps	200
Sierra 185-grain JHP/Unique/1,050 fps	50
Winchester 230-grain SXT	50
Black Hills 230-grain JHP +P	100

Malfunctions: *This unfired pistol suffered a total of seven failures to fully close with the first load, a 230-grain FMJ handload. After 40 rounds break-in was complete. Coupled with the initial stiffness of the controls, we determined that this is a gun held to tight tolerances.*

MODERN HIGH-GRADE COLT, "KEYES PRODUCTION"

This pistol is a stainless Government Model, always a good gun. However, it has three additions to the template that make it a much different pistol. The grips are high-grade walnut and the grip screws are Allen-head rather than the old slot type. The pistol features a long match trigger, which happened to break at a nice 4.5 pounds. Finally, the pistol has forward slide serrations. When I left my friend's shop with this gun, I stuck the gun in my pants, snagging the serrations on my clothing. Still, guns should be carried in a holster and the front serrations are good tools for jacking the slide with gloved hands or when you have less than ideal leverage on the

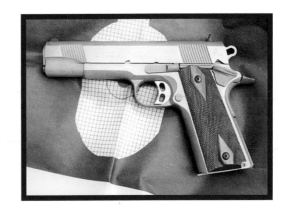

handgun. This pistol showed no break-in malfunctions and gave excellent accuracy. This is probably the best-looking stainless Colt I have seen. The finish was even and well polished, but like many modern Colts was grayer underneath. Overall, it was a good pistol that gave excellent performance.

Controls	E	
Fit and Finish	G	
Trigger	E	(4.5 lbs.)
Sights	G	
Sharp Edges	G	
Overall	G	

Signature Groups:

Cor-Bon 185-grain JHP	2.4 inches
Cor-Bon 230-grain JHP	3.0 inches
Hansen Group: Cor-Bon 200-grain JHP	3.5 inches

Rounds Fired:

Cor-Bon 185-grain JHP	40
Cor-Bon 200-grain JHP	40
Cor-Bon 230-grain JHP	20
Texas Ammunition Tactical 185-grain	100
Powermax 200-grain JHP	100
Black Hills 230-grain JHP +P	100
Hornady 185-grain XTP	50
Hornady 230-grain FP	50

The first 400 rounds were all +Ps — frankly, it was all we had on hand at the time of this test, having expended most of the rounds earmarked for the test program. This makes the gun's performance perhaps even more remarkable.

AUTO ORDNANCE 1911

This is the new version from Khar Arms, and it seems to be improved. Previous AO guns had a well-deserved reputation for internal roughness of parts, but they were worth their modest cost. Sometimes, the internal parts looked as if they had been beaten out on a rock in Pakistan. But the frame and slide, usually Essex parts, were fine. I have had good luck with custom versions that discarded all the rough internal parts. The new AO 1911 worked well enough. It is simply a GI 1911A1, and made to sell at a modest price. It is American made and seems to represent a good value. It

would feed a number of widemouth hollow-points while suffering reasonable break-in malfunctions that were not exhibited by a previous sample. It smoothed in with use and was about as accurate as most GI guns. Overall, while not an exciting gun it was nonetheless a capable one. With a little work, it could outshine the previous AO by a margin –fit and finish are better. It is a good buy considering the modest price and the performance exhibited. I carried this pistol for a time and spent perhaps six months with it. I fitted Ahrends stocks and did away with the plastic factory grips. Let me give Khar a tip – put a decent set of sights on an elevated version and perhaps a better set of stocks and they will have a good carry version of the basic gun. During an experiment with handloads in cold weather, the author fitted the Auto Ordnance .45 with a B Square mount carrying a Bushnell Holosight. The results were simply great. This is a fun combination, offering lightning quick hits and good target acquisition.

Controls	F	
Fit and Finish	G	
Trigger	P	(7.0 lbs.)
Sights	P	
Sharp Edges	F	
Overall	F	

Signature Groups:

Weber 230-grain ball	4.0 inches
Sellier and Bellot ball	4.25 inches
Remington 185-grain Golden Saber +P	4.5 inches
Hansen Group: Sellier and Bellot ball	4.0 inches

Rounds Fired:

Weber ball ammunition	200
Sellier and Bellot ball	100
International Cartridge Frangible	100
Remington Golden Saber 185-grain +P	50
Montana Gold 230-grain JHP/Titegroup/850 fps	50

We had 13 failures to completely go into battery or feed round-nose, ammunition which disappeared after the first 80 rounds.

SPRINGFIELD 1911 A 1

This pistol was an early-model Springfield. It sported a homely set of homemade grips but otherwise was stock. The finish was dull matte, the trigger acceptable, if not great. The pistol is a good example of an early-model Springfield, serviceable but not as highly developed as later models. It would not feed several of the wide-mouth hollow-points, including the Sierra 185-grain JHP, so testing was undertaken with other styles. The ejection port is small, as in military versions.

Previously Fired:	Unknown, used
Controls	F
Fit and Finish	F

Trigger	F	(6.5 lbs)
Sights	P	
Sharp Edges	P	
Overall	F	

Signature Groups:

Star 230-grain RNL	4.0 inches
Star 200-grain SWC	3.8 inches
Hansen Group: Winchester USA ball	5.0 inches

Rounds Fired:

Star 230-grain RNL/231/850 fps	100
Star 200-grain SWC/231/890 fps	100
Winchester USA ball	100
Horandy 200-grain XTP +P*	100
Black Hills 230-grain RNL	50
Federal 230-grain ball**	50

* At this point, the Hornady load would have been the carry load.
** The Federal loads performed well – they were over 30 years old, 1962 boxed military.

At 380 rounds, firing the SWC handloads, we suffered three failures to fully chamber due to accumulated crud in the chamber. The chamber was cleaned at round-count 383 and reliable function was restored.

SPRINGFIELD 1911A1

This is a much newer version. It was found used, and had been fitted with an MGW fixed sight and Hogue grips — the Hogues may have been factory made. The sights were much better than the low-profile GI sights found on 1911A1-type pistols, and offer a notable improvement. The MGW sights are easily fitted and give an excellent sight picture. The Hogue grips were a good addition. This pistol was better finished than the earlier Springfield and featured a larger ejection port, but was definitely a GI-Type gun in appearance. It fed all types of JHP ammunition, an improvement over other pistols. It may cost the most of any GI gun tested, but, in my opinion, it is a good buy. The Springfield 1911A1, in other words, offers much the same quality as the upscale Springfields but has small sights and lacks the custom beavertail safety.

The previous owner of this pistol did one thing — he fitted the MGW sights to this base gun. The grips, as we noted, may have been factory made. In any case, this pistol performed well. It is a great improvement over the early gun. The first Springfield was well made of good material and could have been modified into a real performer. This is a typical basic 1911 with slight improvement that works very well. I understand that the newest 1911A1 Springfields will all have scalloped ejection ports and will sport a better sight, similar to that of the Colt 1991A1. In any case, we had nothing to complain about concerning this handgun.

Controls	G	
Fit and Finish	G	
Trigger	G	(5.25 lbs.)
Sights	G	
Sharp Edges	G	
Overall	G	

Signature Groups:

Winchester ball		4.0 inches
Remington Golden Saber		3.5 inches
Hansen Group:	Speer 185-grain JHP	4.0 inches

Rounds Fired:

Winchester USA ball	100
Remington 230-grain Golden Saber	50
Speer 185-grain JHP	100
Montana Gold 230-grain JHP/Titegroup/850 fps	150
Black Hills 230-grain +P JHP	100

(This is the first time I used Black Hills new +P load, which uses the XTP bullet jolted to 950 fps. This is quite a load, perhaps the best factory load for carry in bear and hog country. It worked well in the Springfield, with perfect feed and good function.)

SPRINGFIELD 1911A1

Roughly comparable to the Colt 1991A1, this Springfield boasts no plastic parts. This pistol has a scalloped or wide ejection port, allowing good administrative handling. The finish was OK, if not great, and the sights were adequate, simply a little larger than those on the military model. The gun may seem ordinary but it is the base gun for the loaded model, and it fed and fired every load we fed it. If you are looking for a reliable defense gun, this is it. The sights are not as good as the MGW sights on another Springfield that we tested, but they are comparable to the Colt 1991A1. Overall, this is a gun that can stand on its own merits.

Previously Fired:	**Less than 100 Rounds: Owner Reported No Malfunctions.**	
Controls	G	
Fit and Finish	G	
Trigger	G	(6.0 lbs.)
Sights	G	
Sharp Edges	G	
Overall	G	

Signature Groups:

Lancer 230-grain Jacketed	4.25 inches
Sellier and Bellot 230-grain ball	4.5 inches
Hansen Group: Black Hills 230-grain JHP +P	4.5 inches

Rounds Fired:

Lancer 230-grain FMJ	150
Sellier and Bellot 230-grain ball	100
Sierra 185-grain JHP/Unique/1,050 fps	100
(Perfect feed with this wide-mouth hollow-point)	
West Coast 185-grain SWC/Plated/Unique/1,100 fps	50
Black Hills 230-grain JHP +P	100

SHORT AUTO ORDNANCE

This is something of a rarity, a Commander-length 1911 produced by Auto Ordnance. I am including it in the military-specification pistols rather than the short .45s because that is exactly what it is, a short GI gun. The short Auto Ordnance guns seem to receive a little extra care. This one sports synthetic grips and high-visibility sights. There were occasional versions of the original Auto Ordnance delivered with good stocks and sights, and this is one of them. Perhaps it was among the last of the original AO production. It is not a bad gun and gave good results. It is roughly comparable to a Series 70 Combat Commander in appearance but with better sights and without the sharp edges seen on some Colts. The fit and

finish are not up to Colt standards, but it is the nicest Auto Ordnance gun
we have seen. It was very quick on target and gave good groups at moderate range. While its 25-yard accuracy was not impressive, the pistol is a
fast fighting gun at short to moderate range.

Controls	G	
Fit and Finish	F	
Trigger	P	**(Consistent but heavy at 8.0 lbs.)**
Sights	G	
Sharp Edges	F	
Overall	G	

Signature Groups:

Winchester Silvertip	4.5 inches
West Coast 230-grain RNP	4.0 inches
Hansen Group: Weber 230-grain ball	4.0 inches

Rounds Fired:

Weber 230-grain Ball	200
Winchester 185-grain Silvertip	50
West Coast 230-grain RN Plated/Accurate # 7/ 850 fps	150
Winchester 230-grain SXT +P	100

Malfunctions - 2; 1 short cycle with Winchester Silvertip; 1 short cycle with West Coast Bullet
load. The gun needs full power, 230-grain loads for good function.

.45 ROCK ISLAND ARMORY 1911

Produced in the Philippines, this is one of my favorite
1911s. I find it to be a good solid pistol faithful to the
1911 template. There were no tool marks and the overall
finish was good, if a little thin, and it picked up gouges
over months of use. The hardwood used for grips is attractive, and the pistol performed well. It is definitely a
good buy. The long trigger and flat mainspring housing
fit most hands well. I am very enthusiastic concerning
this 1911. During the course of evaluations for *Gun
Week, Handguns,* and *Shotgun News,* I fired well over
1,500 rounds with this handgun without a malfunction.

Controls	G	
Fit and Finish	F	
Trigger	F	**(7.0 lbs.)**
Sights	P	
Sharp Edges	F	
Overall	G	

(1,000-round test)

Signature Groups:

Remington ball	3.5 inches
Pro Load 230-grain JHP	3.0 inches
Hansen Group: Remington ball	3.8 inches

Rounds Fired:

Remington UMC ball	400
Pro Load 185-grain JHP	200
Pro Load 200-grain JHP	100
3 D 185-grain JHP	200
Speer 200-grain Gold Dot +P	100

ARGENTINE MODELO 1927

These pistols, produced under license in Argentina, can be good buys. Of late, however, the price has risen for examples. Gunsmiths report difficultly in fitting after-market parts to these pistols — the steel is denser than in the Colt, resulting in an average of one ounce more weight. The pistols appear well made of good material, comparable but not equal to vintage Colt production. Our example would not feed most hollow-point bullet styles and exhibited a heavy trigger action. It exhibited a total of 11 inexplicable malfunctions, all involving a spent case caught in the ejection port. About 100 rounds into the test program, the plastic grips supplied on this refinished pistol cracked and were replaced. Overall, we were not particularly impressed with this gun, but it would be a good base for a custom pistol, as the second version tested shows. Most 1927s display matching serial numbers.

Controls	F	
Fit and Finish	G	
Trigger	P	(8.0 lbs.)
Sights	P	
Overall	F	

Signature Groups:
Zero 230-grain ball	6.1 inches
Winchester 185-grain Silvertip	5.8 inches
Hansen Group: Zero ball	5.6 inches

Rounds Fired:
Zero 230-grain ball	300
Winchester 185-grain Silvertip	50
Sierra 230-grain FMJ/Unique/850 fps	150

ARGENTINE MODELO 1927 CUSTOM

My friends at Dixie Shooter brought this gun up to a much better standard. Purchased from Southern Ohio Gun, the pistol was taken out of the box, examined, and modified without test firing. The trigger was addressed first, and reduced to a nice, crisp 4.0 pounds. The trigger action was a daunting proposition and my friends recommended replacement of the original parts due to their hardness. For economy I used the issue Modelo 1927 as it was. At it turned out, the pistol would drop the hammer on the slide when the slide was dropped on an empty chamber after the trigger action, but never did so when I fired the gun. If you go for a trigger action, use Wilson or Ed Brown parts. The feed ramp was polished and a set of King's Hardballer sights installed. I replaced the cheap plastic grips with a set of nice plastic grips from North Carolina Ordnance. In the end, I had a decent defense pistol that fed every type of ammunition and should prove more than adequate to the task at hand.

Controls	F	
Fit and Finish	E	**(Reblued by Dixie Shooter)**
Trigger	E	**(4.0 lbs.)**
Sights	G	
Sharp Edges	F	
Overall	G	

Signature Groups:

Winchester 230-grain SXT	3.5 inches
Winchester Super X 230-grain FMJ	3.8 inches
Hansen Groups: Winchester Silvertip	4.5 inches

Rounds Fired:

Winchester 230-grain SXT	100
Winchester 230-grain Subsonic	100
Winchester 185-grain Silvertip	100
Winchester Super X 230-grain	100
Sierra 185-grain SWC/Bullseye/950 fps	100

REMINGTON 1911A1

This is an original, well-worn 1911 produced in 1943. It was in fair condition, with a lot of wear and a good, clean barrel. We fired this weapon to see what the gun could do in comparison to modern examples of the breed. It did not fare badly, suffering no malfunctions of any type. Surprisingly, the gun fed, functioned, and performed well with the International Cartridge frangible load. The more we use that load, the more we liked it. The sights were poor, however, and so was the accuracy exhibited by this pistol. Just the same, it would serve to leap into a bunker or clear out a machine-gun nest.

Controls	G	
Fit and Finish	F	
Trigger	G	**(5.0 lbs.)**
Sights	P	
Overall	G	

Signature Groups:

International Cartridge 175-grain	5.6 inches
Fiocchi ball	6.5 inches
Hansen Group:	5.5 inches

Rounds Fired:

International cartridge	50
Fiocchi 230-grain ball	50

.38 SUPER #1

This was an older, well-worn 1911 with much loose motion. Before the firing test, we fitted this pistol with a Kart barrel. Otherwise the loose motion and fit of the barrel would have given poor results. But the pistol has always been reliable with practically any type of load, even though it has rust pits on the slide. The sights are the original type, which limited our tests, but this is a good, reliable defense gun. All testing was done with Triple K magazines. The barrel really got the gun up off its knees. At a later date, sights to complement the barrel will be added.

Controls	F	
Fit and Finish	P	
Sights	P	
Trigger	G	**(4.0 lbs.)**
Sharp Edges	P	
Overall	G	

Signature Groups:

125-grain FP Hunter's Supply/Tite Group/1,050 fps	3.0 inches
115-grain Nosler/Unique/1,366 fps	2.0 inches
Fiocchi 129-grain FMJ/1,233 fps	2.8 inches
Fiocchi Ball	5.6 inches
(Recorded before fitting new barrel)	

Rounds Fired:

FP Hunter's Supply/ Titegroup 125-grain/1050 fps	200
Unique 1150 fps	100
Nosler/Unique 115-grain/1,366 fps	100
Fiocchi 129-grain/1,233 fps	100

.38 SUPER #2

This is an original gun in nice condition, included to show what the stock originals were capable of. It was more accurate than these guns are sometimes given credit for. The first Super was doing 4–6 inches before being fitted with a new barrel. This is a fine defense gun just as it is, but would be improved by a new barrel.

Controls	G	
Fit and Finish	E	
Sights	F	
Trigger	G	(5.0 lbs.)
Sharp Edges	F	
Overall	G	

Signature Groups:

Cor-Bon 115-grain JHP	3.75 inches
Fiocchi 129-grain FMJ	3.6 inches

Rounds Fired:

Cor-Bon 115-grain JHP	20
W W 115-grain FMJ/231/1,199 fps	80
Fiocchi 129-grain FMJ	50
Remington UMC 130-grain FMJ	50

ROCK ISLAND ARMORY .38 SUPER

Everything that applies to the RIA .45 applies to this weapon, except that the .38 Supers are delivered with a slide that features an enlarged ejection port. This pistol handled as well or better than the original Colts, with excellent fit and no tool marks visible in disassembly. Overall, that is a good solid pistol in a fine caliber.

Controls	G	
Fit and Finish	F	
Trigger	G	(5.0 lbs.)
Sights	P	
Sharp Edges	F	
Overall	G	

Signature Groups:

Winchester 130-grain ball	4.5 inches
Ranier 124-grain JHP	4.0 inches
Hansen Group: Winchester ball	3.0 inches

Rounds Fired:

Winchester 120-grain ball	50
Federal 147-grain ball	50
Winchester Silvertip	50
Remington 130-grain ball	50
Remington 115-grain JHP	100
Ranier 124-grain JHP/Unique/1,360 fps	250

The pistol exhibited several odd malfunctions. It would not feed ball ammunition if the magazine was fully loaded, but downloading to seven rounds cured this problem. We used McCormack, MecGar, and Triple magazines with the same results. Even Metalform did not properly load. Once loaded the gun did fine. After 250, this first round malfunction disappeared. It was never present in cases loaded with the Hornady TJ case. The factory loads are loaded too short, we believe, and the handloader can make the most of this caliber.

ROCK ISLAND ARMORY #2

This is the same pistol, but deserving of a new test period by virtue of several beneficial modifications. We fitted a set of McCormack sights. These sights fit into the existing dovetail and offer a much better sight picture. With the existing front sight, the gun shot high at moderate range and dead-on at 50 yards. This will be addressed by a new front sight in the future. The safety was replaced with a drop safety from Brownells. Racy and effective, this is a fine addition to the .38 Super. We also replaced the fair original grips with a beautiful set from Esmeralda O'Sheehan. This really set the pistol off. Best of all, we carefully fitted a Nowlin match-grade barrel.

We had our top flight .38 Super. After adjusting the trigger to a smooth 3.0 pounds, the pistol did not resemble the original in performance. This is a good solid handgun.

Signature Groups:

Ranier Load 124-grain	1.9 inches
Sierra Load 115-grain	2.4 inches
XTP Load 115-grain	2.65 inches
Cor-Bon 115-grain JHP	2.5 inches

Hansen Group: Ranier Load   4.0 inches

Rounds Fired:

124-grain Ranier JHP/Unique/1,370 fps	250
115-grain Ranier JHP/Titegroup/1,190 fps	150
115-grain Sierra JHP/Herco/1,355 fps	200
115-grain Nosler JHP/231/1,390 fps	200
Cor-Bon 115-grain JHP	50
Zero JHP 115-grain	50
Fiocchi FMJ 129-grain	50

KIMBER TARGET MODEL

This Kimber Target version gave overwhelmingly good results. We discovered two things about the Super during the course of firing 2,500 rounds through the Kimber over a period of approximately six months. First, the Super is inexpensive to feed and, second, it's very easy to shoot well. After a simple cleaning, the pistol showed little sign of the large number of rounds that had been put through it. The Kimber never suffered a malfunction of

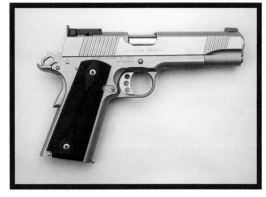

any type. It performed brilliantly during our test. The gun is fitted tightly for accuracy but not so tightly that it will fail to function properly.

The Target model must be aimed properly and carefully. As a target version the gun has a bit more weight than some 1911s, and while some of the lighter guns allow for much quicker shooting, the Kimber makes up for its heft with superb accuracy. This was a surprise because the Super usually is not as accurate as a comparable .45. The Super responded well to handloads and is a thoroughly modern 1911, well suited to the Super cartridge. For someone who needs more penetration than the average offered by a .45, or who is simply a Super enthusiast, this is the ultimate 1911. I would not change a thing on this pistol. In point of fact I carried it often in my High Noon shoulder holster as my personal defense weapon. I cannot give a higher compliment.

Controls	E	
Fit and Finish	E	
Trigger	E	(4.0 lbs.)
Sights	E +	
Sharp Edges	G	
Overall	E	

Signature Groups:

Gold Dot/231/124-grain/1,250 fps	1.0 inch
Ranier/231/115-grain/1,300 fps	1.25 inch
Cor-Bon 115-grain JHP	2.0 inches
Remington UMC 130-grain FMJ	3.0 inches
Hansen Group: Zero JHP	3.0 inches

Rounds Fired:

Remington UMC 130-grain FMJ	400
Winchester USA 130-grain FMJ	300
Fiocchi 129-grain FMJ	300
Federal American Eagle 147-grain	200
Zero 115-grain JHP	200
Georgia Arms 147-grain JHP	50
Mullins Custom 124-grain XTP	50
Gold Dot/231/115-grain/1,250 fps	400
Ranier/231/115-grain/1,300 fps	100
XTP/Unique/124-grain/1,350 fps	100
XTP/Titegroup/124-grain/1,290 fps	100
Nosler JHP/Titegroup/115-grain	250
Winchester FMJ/231/115-grain/190 fps	50

COLT SERIES 80 STAINLESS ENHANCED MODEL, .40 CALIBER SMITH & WESSON

This pistol is as good a gun on its own merits as any modern Colt tested. I am not personally a fan of the .40-caliber Smith & Wesson cartridge, but I am told there are many police jurisdictions that allow officers "any handgun, .40 caliber" and the Colt is popular. In certain competitions the .40 offers advantages. For use in the Colt the .40 cartridge can be long-loaded for good accuracy and power with a minimum of pressure. The technique is to seat the bullet farther out in the case.

In our test we fired this pistol a lot, and with only two spare magazines! Despite my expectation that the short round would give problems, the pistol did quite well. This Colt is a pre-Keyes gun and has a fairly rough finish. With a mean streak, I liberally dosed it with Pro Tech oil and did not clean or lubricate the gun until it had fired 1,100 rounds. Even then it did not malfunction. Overall, the gun did well. For those who believe in the .40-caliber, this is the top choice.

Signature Groups:

Sellier and Bellot Ball	4.0 inches
Black Hills 155-grain JHP	3.0 inches
Cor-Bon 135-grain JHP	3.4 inches
Hansen Group: Cor-Bon 135-grain JHP	3.0 inches

Rounds Fired:

Sellier and Bellot Ball	500
TJ Coneveras Frangible	500
Black Hills 155-grain JHP	100
Cor-Bon 135-grain JHP	100
Fiocchi 170-grain MAJOR	50

The frangible loads are available as an inexpensive option from T. J. Coneveras, a respected police supplier who also stocks the Sellier and Bellot ball used in much of this work.

COLT DELTA ELITE 10MM

This is an older blued gun in good shape. I think that the pistol has potential, but I ran into one troublesome consideration. Colonel Jeff Cooper felt that the 10mm had better long-range performance than the .45, but when attempting 50- to 100-yard off-hand shots, the recoil was so stout that it was necessary to hold the sights below the target in order to connect. In other words, recoil caused the pistol to shoot high at long range, rather than low. The muzzle flip was fairly consistent but not pleasant. The Delta's accuracy at moderate range was good. This gun has a reputation for early wear with full-power loads, but with heavy W. C. Wolff springs wound over a Hartt's Recoil Reducer, we think we have made a big improvement over the factory version. No discernable wear was recorded after 500 trouble-free rounds. At moderate range, the pistol is controllable. While the 10mm has done well in the hunting field, overall I see little reason to choose this caliber over a .45 ACP.

Controls	E	
Fit and Finish	E	
Trigger	G	(4.5 lbs.)
Sights	G	
Sharp Edges	F	
Overall	G	

Signature Groups:

Hornady 180-grain XTP	2.0 inches
Hornady 200-grain FP	2.5 inches

Rounds Fired:

Hornady 180-grain XTP	200
Hornady 200-grain XTP	100
Hornady 200-grain FP/Unique/1,100 fps	100
Winchester 175-grain Silvertip	100

RIA/9MM

I was unable to secure a 9mm 1911 type pistol — but then, I didn't look very hard. In the spirit of testing as many calibers as possible, I ordered a simple Colt-type 9mm barrel from Brownell and plugged it into a .38 Super Rock Island Armory gun. The breech face of the Super is larger than that of the 9mm and sometimes the Super extractor could be expected not to work, but in our test it worked fine. I used Triple K magazines, 9mm Luger Specific. My firing impression was good. The 9mm 1911 is docile and easy to use well. I still see the caliber as best used in practice for the Super, but just the same, the results were good. I am certain a factory gun would perform even better than my lash-up.

Ratings: See RIA .38 Super
Signature Groups:

Uzi 9mm Die Cut JHP	4.5 inches
Handload	4.25 inches

Rounds Fired:

Uzi 115-grain JHP	200
Uzi 115-grain Black Tip	200
Handload 124-grain XTP/Unique/1,100 fps	100

We went to Paul Cole of Cole Distributing for genuine IMI ammunition. The Die Cut hollow-point had previously shown excellent accuracy and expansion. We also used the awesome black-tip Uzi load.

COLT 1991A1 WITH .400 COR-BON BARREL

Wanting to give the .400 Cor-Bon a good test, I fitted a KKM barrel in standard five-inch length to a modified 1911. The barrel fit perfectly, but I did have to open up the magazine lips slightly to ensure good feeding and, after a bit of experimentation, the magazines worked fine. The .400 Cor-Bon offers plenty of velocity and good accuracy. It shoots flatter than the .45 but also offers more recoil. If you decide upon the .400 Cor-Bon as a carry-gun cartridge, you can practice with the original barrel and magazines. In addition, brass is becoming easier to get and handloading the .400 Cor-Bon is not particularly difficult. Modifications of this nature do not always work well but in this case they did. With the 150-grain loads, the pistol fired to the point of aim.

Ratings–See 1991A1 pistol with improvements.

Signature Group:

Cor-Bon 150-grain	2.0 inches
Cor-Bon 135-grain	2.25 inches
Hansen Group: Cor-Bon 135-grain	4.5 inches

Rounds Fired:

Cor-Bon 135-grain	140
Cor-Bon 150-grain	40
Cor-Bon 165-grain	40

POLICE PISTOLS

THE KIMBER ULTRA CARRY

This pistol is the most popular pistol chosen by the men and women of the Tacoma, Washington, police department. The Kimber Ultra Carry's four-inch barrel is a new paradigm in the 1911, a bit shorter than a Commander, but with a longer barrel than the officer's model. Ammunition performance was good in terms of accuracy and a full powder burn, but the velocity loss was marked. A typical 870 fps 230-grain JHP was reduced to about 790 fps from the four-inch Ultra Carry barrel. In any case, the .45 relies upon sectional density and frontal mass for performance, not velocity. In ballistic gelatin or wet newsprint testing, the loss of expansion was slight.

Like all Kimbers, this handgun was completely reliable. The sights are simply great, and I did not miss front slide serrations on this pistol. The trigger broke as cleanly as any Kimber and the firing session went well. Like many short-barrel .45s you have to concentrate to get hits but this pistol gave excellent results. Overall, the Kimber is an excellent short .45. I found myself shooting a little low with this gun, and had it been my personal gun I would have fitted an arched mainspring housing. This is an ideal police pistol and a good choice for anything except hunting, which requires a longer sight radius and better velocity. When using this pistol the results were very near those obtained with longer-slide handguns. The Ultra Carry was very fast into action, even using a Commander-length holster.

Controls	E	
Fit and Finish	G	
Trigger	E	(3.0 lbs.)
Sharp Edges	G	
Overall	E	

Signature Groups:

PMC 230-grain ball	4.25 inches
PMC 230-grain Starfire	4.0 inches
Hansen Groups: Aguila, 230-grain FMJ	3.9 inches

Rounds Fired:

PMC 230-grain ball	300
Aquila 230-grain ball	100
MC 230-grain Starfire	100

ARMSCORPS MEDALLION

This is quite an interesting gun. It is an elevated version of the pistols produced by Armsor in the Philippines. The pistol is finished in a deep, rich blue to rival anything Colt has ever done. The pistol is well put together, with excellent fit and finish and good polish of all parts. The pistol features a slide that departs considerably from the 1911 template. The slide has front and rear cocking serrations and a trough running through the bottom of the slide connecting the serrations. The effect is pleasing, and the trough is well polished. The pistol features a fiber-optic front sight. And the rear sight

is fully adjustable. The adjustable sights have square posts that are beveled, and the sights are smoothed-out. The gun is supplied with an adjustment tool that aids in making incremental adjustments, and the sights hold the zero under the pounding of heavy-duty ammunition. No break-in malfunctions of any kind were experienced.

The pistol features an ambidextrous safety, and the grip safety is a well-designed type that features well executed checkering. The mainspring housing has the same checkering all of which, while machined, has the look of hand checkering. The trigger compression was very nice and crisp at four pounds even. After firing a bit it became smoother. The pistol's grips are topflight Pachmayr rubber. The Medallion was supplied with two magazines. The pistol's full-length guide rod is always debatable, but if you do not like the guide rod, you can remove it. When a pistol shoots accurately with a full-length guide rod, however, it should probably be left in the weapon! The Medallion is free of sharp edges and shows excellent attention to detail. It is a good buy. The only question might be, "Will it hold up in hard use?" The template is a good one and guns from the same factory have given good service. The test is very encouraging. This is an excellent pistol for IDPA, personal defense, or even hunting.

Controls	**E**	
Fit and Finish	**E**	
Sights	**E**	
Trigger	**G**	**(4.0 lbs., /settled in at 3.8 lbs.)**
Sharp Edges	**G**	
Overall	**G**	

Signature Groups:

Winchester Silvertip	3.5 inches
Federal 230-grain Hydra Shock	3.0 inches
Weber 230-grain ball	2.9 inches

Rounds Fired:

Weber 230-grain ball	350
Winchester Silvertip	50
Federal 230-grain Hydra Shock	50
Triton 165-grain JHP +P	50

RESULTS

When all was said and done we had separated weapons performance into neat little columns. We had on hand as many as five 1911s at one time and wished to do a shootout as a measure of their ability. We succumbed to a bench-rest accuracy test largely because some of the guns were so accurate we became intensely interested. But we also did a combat shootout, based on several parameters. In the end, in this final shootout, there were no losers, but we saw pistols that exhibited excellent performance.

Pistols:
Kimber Custom II
High Standard G Man
Colt Commander

We performed three drills. We drew and fired at a seven-yard target and fired a single shot. Then we performed the Bill Drill, seven shots as quickly as possible at seven yards. Finally we performed the Hansen drill again. The target used at seven yards and for the Bill Drill was the Gibson pepper popper. Since the distance was close, we used the excellent frangible ammunition offered by T J Coneveras. Using bullets of about 150 grains at 1,040 fps, this is an accurate and safe load for training with steel targets. The Commander simply lapt into my hand and took out the targets. It is that kind of gun. The longer guns performed better at longer range and when more control was needed. The winner? The Commander is a splendid combat gun, the others a bit easier to use well in rapid fire. All are excellent guns. The Bill Drill is usually fired at a paper target; having to hit the popper each time naturally was harder and will make for slower times than often recorded.

Gun	Times (one shot /seven yards)	Bill Drill	Hansen Drill
Colt Commander	92	1.7	4.0 inches
High Standard G Man	1.01	.64	3.25 inches
Kimber Custom II	1.06	1.5	3.2 inches

ABSOLUTE ACCURACY

This was a tough test with many variables. We chose three of the most accurate guns and our most accurate loadings. These are recorded. All results are more than acceptable but we think that the high-end guns are definitely worth their price to the accuracy maven. We shot these groups with four proven loadings off a solid benchrest, firing 15 rounds of each load and recording the average. These pistols are good, accurate enough for any type of competition. Twenty-five-yard groups were measured from inside of each bullet hole to the other, in the farthest spaced-holes.

Load One	230-grain XTP	Titegroup 850 fps	Loaded by John Miller
Load Two	230-grain Montana Gold	Unique 809 fps	Loaded by R K Campbell and Bobbie Ann Campbell
Load Three	Federal 230-grain	MATCH	
Load Four	Winchester 230-grain	SXT	

Gun	Load One	Load Two	Load Three	Load Four	Average
Wilson Combat CQB	1.9 inches	2.5 inches	2.4 inches	2.0 inches	2.2 inches
Kimber Custom II	1.75 inches	2.0 inches	2.15 inches	2.5 inches	2.1 inches
High Stanard G Man	1.6 inches	2.5 inches	1.9 inches	2.6 inches	2.15 inches
Springfield Stainless w/ Nowlin barrel	2.2 inches	2.9 inches	2.3 inches	2.6 inches	2.5 inches

LOADS USING UNIQUE POWDER

During the course of the past 25 years, I have developed a number of loads that use Unique powder. Introduced at the turn of the century, Unique is among the most established powders in the world. I have used both moderate and high-end loads with good results. The maximum loads should be approached with caution, beginning at least 10 percent below maximum powder charge. Use these loads only in quality weapons. I have enjoyed good results. Pay close attention to overall length in loading and use this data at your own risk. Unique is not the cleanest powder, but generally gives good to excellent results. For many years it was the only powder I used.

Powder charge	Bullet	Velocity	Comments
5.6 grains	West Coast 185-grain	690 fps	Too light to function in some pistols, very mild and accurate
5.7 grains	West Coast 185-grain	701 fps	Better function
5.8 grains	Hornady 185-grain XTP	707 fps	Accurate
7.0 grains	Sierra 185-grain JHP	805 fps	Small-game load
7.3 grains	Hornady 185-grain XTP	867 fps	
7.5 grains	Sierra 185-grain JHP	1,014 fps	Good small game
8.0 grains	Nosler 185-grain JHP	1,030 fps	Good expansion
7.3 grains	Speer 200-grain Gold Dot	956 fps	Accurate
7.5 grains	Hornady 200-grain XTP	960 fps	Accurate
6.5 grains	Sierra 230-grain FMJ	859 fps	
7.0 grains	Sierra 230-grain JHP	894 fps	
7.0 grains	Hornady 230-grain XTP	876 fps	Accurate
7.2 grains	Speer 230-grain Gold Dot	939 fps	Heavy load
7.2 grains	Sierra 230-grain JHP	922 fps	Accurate

DIFFERENCES IN VELOCITY IN BARREL LENGTHS

During the course of the test, we took many velocity readings. There is a significant difference in the powder burn in 3.5-/4.25- and 5.0-inch barrel lengths. We think most readers will find the results interesting. These are average results given in feet per second from several pistols.

Load	5" barrel	4.25" barrel	3.5" barrel
Cor-Bon 165-grain JHP	1211	1149	
Federal 165-grain Personal Defense	1005	1050	1001
Speer 185-grain Gold Dot	1044	948	842
Remington 185-grain JHP	1004	953	
Remington 185-grain JHP+P	1130	1067	
Cor-Bon 200-grain JHP	1090	1054	1001
Gold Dot 200-grain +P	1040	980	
Black Hills 230-grain JHP+P	947	875	823
Hornady 230-grain XTP+P	931	880	
Speer 230-grain Gold Dot	841	820	768
Remington 230-grain Golden Saber	870	824	739

All velocities were recorded by a Competition Electronics Chronograph

SHOOTOUT

We took the Rock Island GI gun and the Medallion, made within a few years of the other but separated by generations in features, to the range. We wanted to see how improved the modern guns are over GI guns. Well, in short range, with down and dirty shooting at three to nine yards, one was as good as the other. As soon as the sights became important, however, the Medallion stole the show. The trigger action was also important in bench-rest accuracy.

25-YARD GROUPS

Ammunition	RIA GI Gun	Medallion
Weber 230-grain ball	4.0 inches	2.5 inches
Black Hills 230-grain RNL	4.2 inches	3.0 inches
Black Hills 185-grain JHP	4.5 inches	2.0 inches
Remington 230-grain Golden Saber	3.8 inches	3.2 inches
Sierra 230-grain JHP/Titegroup	3.0 inches	1.9 inches

The Medallion is well fitted but sights mean a lot, so does trigger compression. And our hands were much less tired after handling this gun for a few runs on the target. This modern 1911 is a much better gun than anything we had in the past. The RIA would serve in most any role related to home defense, however, and a good point to be made of this test program is that there were no malfunctions!

SPECIAL EQUIPMENT USED DURING OUR TESTS:

Hansen Eagle Eye Shooting Glasses

These glasses protect the eye from injury and harsh light and also have a bifocal component that allows less-than-perfect eyes to focus on handgun sights. A must-have.

The RCBS Trigger Pull Gauge

Compact and affordable, we could not have tested trigger compression without this handy tool.

RCBS Loading Gear

From the press to the Little Dandy powder measure, we used RCBS throughout the test program.

Starline Brass

We could never have had so many first-class loads made up in time for testing without Starline — particularly in .38 Super!

Walker Game Ears

Top-notch hearing protection. These muffs block out offensive sound but allow normal conversation to enter, essential for range safety and communication.

Shoot N C Targets

These bright targets made the shooting day go faster.

Birchwood Casey Oil

This well-known and respected lubricant kept our 1911s running.

Hoppes Solvent and Uncle Mike's Targets

Hoppes solvent was used in the majority of cleaning chores, and more than a little of it! We could not have used anything more effective in this type of test. The Uncle Mike's targets really helped with those aging eyes, again!

.22 CALIBER CONVERSION UNITS

THE WILSON COMBAT CONVERSION UNIT

This is a tremendous training aid and a recreational jewel, and I think it is among the best-made devices ever constructed for the 1911. Early versions from Colt used a floating chamber and were known to lead poorly at times. The Wilson Combat unit is free from this problem. I have fired over 3,000 rounds in this unit with perhaps only a dozen malfunctions of various types, usually failures to fully chamber. In use, .22-caliber rimfire ammunition is neither as rugged nor as fail safe as centerfire ammunition. My verison is fitted with Wilson Combat low-profile sights. The fit and finish are a good complement to any .45. I have used this conversion on Springfield, Colt, and Wilson guns with perfect function.

Controls	NA
Fit and Finish	E
Trigger	NA
Sights	E
Sharp Edges	G
Overall	E

Signature Groups*:
Winchester Wildcat	2.0 inches
Winchester Dynapoint	2.25 inches
Hansen drill, Dynapoints	1.9 inches

Rounds Fired:
Winchester Wildcat	1,000
Winchester Dynapoint	1,000
Wolff	500
Aguila High Speed	400
Aguila 60-grain Subonic	100

Signature groups are fired when mounted on a Wilson Combat CQB

The Aguila High Speed load is dynamite. The 60-grain Subsonic keyholes often — it is really meant for long-barrel rifles — but it keyholes accurately! It is fun to shoot and that is what it is all about. (Some were uncounted in recreational shooting, an oversight. We counted empty bricks to give an accurate count. We cleaned this unit approximately every 500 rounds.)

CIENER .22 CALIBER CONVERSION UNIT

This is the platinum version, intended to give target-grade accuracy. When used with a weapon with a good trigger, the Ciener does indeed deliver. We achieved a number of sub-one-inch groups at 15 yards and several hovering at the one-inch mark at 25 yards. The large target sights are much easier to pick up quickly than most handgun sights. This unit is well finished and reliability was on a par with the Wilson unit, with the usual disturbances due to the quality variances of .22-caliber ammunition. I have fired perhaps 2,000 rounds in the Ciener, with a dozen malfunctions or so. All of the malfunctions of the Ceiner were recorded during the first 500 rounds. After that, function was flawless, including a run of 800 rounds without cleaning. One warning — do not purchase this unit without ordering at least one spare magazine. It is too much fun to be without a spare!

Fit and Finish	E
Sights	E
Sharp Edges	P
(Due to sights — very unfair for a target pistol but we stick to the combat-type ratings.)	
Overall	E

Signature Groups:

Winchester Wildcat	2.5 inches
Winchester T 22	1.0 inches
Remington Thunderbolt	1.5 inches

Hansen Group: Remington Yellowjacket   2.0 inches

Rounds Fired

Winchester Wildcat	500
Winchester T 22	100
Remington Thunderbolt	1,000
Remington Yellowjacket	300
Remington Standard Velocity	100

KIMBER .22 CALIBER CONVERSION UNIT.

This is a well-made unit, an obvious good match to the Kimber pistol. I borrowed it from a reluctant owner and was allowed to test a mere 100 rounds — followed by an immediate cleaning! I didn't mind, but I would have enjoyed testing the conversion further. In limited testing I experienced no malfunctions, and the unit had fewer than 500 breaks in rounds in service. The Kimber Target .22 caliber conversion unit differs in details from the others with a target sight and front slide serrations.

Fit and Finish	E	
Sights	E	
Sharp Edges	P	**(Due to sights!!!)**

Signature Group:

Remington Thunderbolt	1.4 inches
No Hansen fired:	

FITTED ON KIMBER CUSTOM II
Rounds Fired

Remington Thunderbolt	100

SUMMARY

After this test program and the research on the 1911, I stand even more in awe of this magnificent pistol. The 1911 is still in frontline service, saving the lives of good men and women all over the world. Just last week I saw a photo of an Israeli officer clearing a tunnel under a city with a 1911 pistol in hand. To service personnel in many parts of the world, a 1911 pistol represents a tremendous individual expense, but fighting men will go the extra mile and sacrifice other gear to deploy the 1911. I have seen the 1911 carried in shoulder holsters by men issued lesser weapons, and seen others carry the pistol against regulation at risk of official reprimand.

I am still anxious to see what the future brings for the 1911. The story of the 1911 is far from over, and I suspect in a few years someone will be looking at this book and find that it is outdated in some manner. Beyond a shadow of a doubt, new 1911s will be introduced during the next few years. They may have new features and various engineering improvements to make them easier to manufacture, more durable, more accurate, or even more comfortable to fire, but they will still be 1911s. Nothing has dulled my enthusiasm for the 1911 — quite the contrary. This experience has solidified my faith in the greatest American pistol.

MODEL
1911
MODEL
1911
MODEL
1911
MODEL
1911
MODEL
1911
MODEL
1911
MODEL
1911
MODEL
1911
MODEL
1911
MODEL
1911
MODEL
1911
MODEL
1911
MODEL
1911
MODEL
1911
MODEL
1911
MODEL
1911
MODEL
1911
MODEL
1911
MODEL
1911
MODEL
1911
MODEL
1911
MODEL
1911
MODEL
1911
MODEL
1911
MODEL
1911
MODEL
1911
MODEL
1911
MODEL
1911
MODEL
1911
MODEL
1911
MODEL
1911

Special thanks to Dixie Gun Works for photos on pages; 7, 14